May you be blessed as you read!

Olivia Davenport
1 Corinthians 2:5

Love
Magnified

Uncovering the Love Story
in
God's Word

OLIVIA DAVENPORT

WESTBOW
P R E S S°
A DIVISION OF THOMAS NELSON
& ZONDERVAN

This book is a work of non-fiction. Unless otherwise noted, the author and the publisher make no explicit guarantees as to the accuracy of the information contained in this book and in some cases, names of people and places have been altered to protect their privacy.

WestBow Press books may be ordered through booksellers or by contacting:

WestBow Press
A Division of Thomas Nelson & Zondervan
1663 Liberty Drive
Bloomington, IN 47403
www.westbowpress.com
844-714-3454

Because of the dynamic nature of the Internet, any web addresses or links contained in this book may have changed since publication and may no longer be valid. The views expressed in this work are solely those of the author and do not necessarily reflect the views of the publisher, and the publisher hereby disclaims any responsibility for them.

Unless otherwise indicated, all Scripture taken from the New King James Version®. Copyright © 1982 by Thomas Nelson. Used by permission. All rights reserved.

Scripture quotations marked (NLT) are taken from the Holy Bible, New Living Translation, copyright ©1996, 2004, 2015 by Tyndale House Foundation. Used by permission of Tyndale House Publishers, Carol Stream, Illinois 60188. All rights reserved.

Scripture quotations marked (ESV) are from the ESV® Bible (The Holy Bible, English Standard Version®), copyright © 2001 by Crossway, a publishing ministry of Good News Publishers. Used by permission. All rights reserved.

ISBN: 978-1-6642-2546-6 (sc)
ISBN: 978-1-6642-2548-0 (hc)
ISBN: 978-1-6642-2547-3 (e)

Library of Congress Control Number: 2021903992

Print information available on the last page.

WestBow Press rev. date: 03/08/2021

Dedicated to my audience of One, in whom
I live, move and have my being

Even though the fig trees have no blossoms, and there are no grapes on the vines; even though the olive crop fails, and the fields lie empty and barren; even though the flocks die in the fields, and the cattle barns are empty, yet I will rejoice in the Lord! I will be joyful in the God of my salvation!
Habakkuk 3:17–18 (NLT)

CONTENTS

THANKFUL, GRATEFUL, BLESSED ACKNOWLEDGEMENTS

The completion of this book comes not from my own efforts and impetus, but through being obedient to the gentle prompting and encouragement of God's Holy Spirit. He walked with me through every page. For that I thank Abba, my heavenly Father, who knows all things and goes before me in every endeavor. All praise, all honor, and all glory belong to Him alone.

Whatever the endeavor, my family never fails to support. They are my own cheerleading squad. This project has been no different. Thank you, Walter, for the quiet support and helpful confidence that you give me as I work. You have never complained about a missed meal; that blesses me and frees me to do what I do. Inga, J.C., Mechele, and Jessica, thank you for your unequivocal support of all my efforts. Jalen McMiller, owner of Abstract Productions KC, thank you for the best headshots. You perfectly captured Grandma in all her moods! I pray each of you will read and be blessed. I love you more.

Many others have come alongside me on this journey, offering encouragement, insight and specific expertise as I worked. This book is a perfect example of 1 Corinthians 12:7–11, many members, many gifts, all being used to bring our heavenly Father glory. Thank you, Pastor Stan Archie, for your input regarding organization and learning outcomes. Your support is important. Thanks also go to my Christian Fellowship Baptist Church family. You were my first audience for this book, studying it through the season of Lent 2020, offering encouragement and feedback. Thank you. I love serving with you; each year becomes more precious.

Thank you to the editors who read and re-read the book for me. There were two sets of editors for this project: those who read it as it was being readied as a devotional for the 2020 Lent season, and those who read it as it was being readied for publication. I thank each of you: Jessica Thomas,

Scott and Dawnita Phillips, Jamelle Brown, Tracey Roland, Quinn and Amber Tolbert. Your insights were invaluable.

It is a special treasure and a balm for my heart to know that I am covered in prayer by many as I write. It has been an extra special blessing to have you come alongside me and write prayers for this book. You could never know how your prayers, written for the readers of this book, also blessed me. Thank you, Evelyn Archie, Marquita Jacks, Dawnita Phillips, Katrina Case, Charity Brown-Ritchie, Valencia Griswold, Vernita Askew, James Edwards, Tracey Roland, and Jessica Thomas. Rebecca Edwards, my own prayer partner, went home to be with the Lord shortly after writing her prayer. I miss you my dear sister. Thank you for the many prayers we prayed together and for the one you wrote for this book.

There were times when I procrastinated and there were times when life genuinely delayed this project. I specifically want to thank those of you who came alongside and quietly asked about 'the book.' That encouragement pushed me to completion, but it also surprised me and made me smile. I smiled because it was good to know that someone was waiting to hear what God had to say and believed in my ability to write it. You know who you are. Thank you.

With gratitude and love,
Olivia D.

We love because he
first loved us.

———

1 JOHN 4:19 (ESV)

BEFORE YOU BEGIN

God loves you. I am sure you've heard that many times. Perhaps while you were wandering around a mall, someone came up and shared a message about God's love for you. Maybe you heard it at a church service, or maybe you heard it during a time of grief or loss. Either way, we have all been told that God loves us. Especially at a time of loss, the truth of that statement may not have resonated with you. Perhaps you heard it and kept moving, or maybe you paused and filed it away for another time. Whatever your response, the truth of that statement never changes. God loves you: today, tomorrow, always.

As you begin these days of study and devotion, be forewarned: it is my intent that at the end you will have developed a special sense of His love for you. I pray that you will be overwhelmed by His love and all that He has done to prove His love for you. I pray that after you finish these days of devotion, whenever you pick up your Bible, you will be especially sensitive to the fact that from Genesis to Revelations, the Holy Bible is truly one big love letter to you from God. May you know unquestionably His heart for you.

This truth about God's love for you comes with a question: How will you respond to His love? Your response will not dampen His love. His love is above and beyond what we experience with people. It is unconditional, unquenchable, and never failing. Your response, however, will determine whether you are able to experience the joy of His unconditional, unquenchable love. Your response will determine whether you will be able to share His love with others.

You will see, hear, and experience God's love most when you are still. The noise and activity of our world jangles our nerves and causes us to react to the urgent, but not the important. His love is important. It is important to the proper functioning of our Spirit. We are told in scripture that "God is Spirit, and those who worship Him must worship in spirit and truth" (John 4:24). His Spirit, connecting with us at times when we are open to hearing His voice, quiets us and allows us to be enveloped with His presence and experience the power of His love and care.

On some level, I question the audacity of writing about God's love because it is so much bigger than anything we can imagine with our finite minds. But, in our diseased world, we very much need a reminder that there is one place that remains unchanging, because it is inhabited by the God who is unchanging and dares to love us in spite of ourselves and in spite of where we have taken the world that He created for us.

His love follows us every day. All day long He seeks us. On the surface His love may look like the blundering love of a lovesick teen, unrequited but ever faithful. However, when we tear apart the rose and examine it in detail, we will be blown away by the fact that all day long we are followed around by the love of the all-powerful, all-knowing, all-seeing, ever present God who yearns for us to acknowledge Him as Lord and Savior in what may seem to us like the most insignificant details of our lives.

We have become used to love stories that can be captured in a two-hour segment on television or at the movies. God's love story cannot be captured and dismissed so easily. It begins, for our capacities, in Genesis - although for God, it started before the foundation of the world. For those who choose to know Him, this love story has no end. This love story is an ongoing epic that transcends this life and takes us into eternity with Him. We cannot imagine a love so great that it knows no bounds, has no end.

From Genesis to Revelation, we are given glimpses of this great love – this love He has for you and me. I invite you to share the true stories of His love through the pages of His word, the Holy Bible. Meet some of the people who were changed by His love and came to know Him so that you too may walk with Him and experience the most powerful love known to man – the love that will transform you from the inside out.

I'd like for you to be intentional about this study. Decide now to finish each day, even if you need to devote extra time to get it done. Let these days of devotion reach down into your heart. Pay attention to the learning outcomes for each section. Grab a pencil and spend some time each day answering the questions and journaling and meditating about what the Holy Spirit brings to mind. For these days, allow the importance of God's words to speak louder than the urgent matters at hand.

Let's start at the beginning …

THEY HAVE PRAYED FOR YOU

Because it is my intention for you to know how much God loves you, I have prayed for you. I've also asked others to pray for you as you begin reading lessons from scripture that uncover God's love for you. I echo the prayer of the Apostle Paul from Ephesians: "that the God of our Lord Jesus Christ, the Father of glory, may give to you the spirit of wisdom and revelation in the knowledge of Him, (Ephesians 1:17). In His Name, Amen.

They have prayed for you:

Heavenly Father, Holy and Righteous You are! We trust Your unfailing love to ignite the hearts of all who will read these words, that You give wisdom and clarity by Your Spirit. Transform hearts, stir up gifts as we walk this journey serving You Lord for the building of Your Kingdom.

Evelyn A., Kansas City, MO

Father God, You created everything! We stand in awe of You and Your creation. You know everything! We stand in need of Your wisdom, moment by moment, day by day. We come to You desiring to know more about You and more about ourselves through You. Teach us to trust You more. Please keep us from leaning to our own understanding. As we commit to this journey, we offer our bodies as living sacrifices to You. Holy Spirit open our hearts and minds to receive the gift of knowledge that You have for us. Convict and confirm us. Rebuke and comfort us by Your Word. Teach us Your ways so that what we learn goes far past the pages of this book and far past these days, as we seek to grow in a life that worships and pleases You. Lord, we thank You for the godly wisdom, insight, transparency and obedience of sister Olivia in sharing what You've given her with the rest of the world through this devotional. We expect to hear from You O' God!

We expect to be blessed with the newness of discovery and revelation. Bless and keep us all. In the precious and matchless name of Jesus. Amen.

Marquita J., Kansas City, MO

Jesus, You are Who so many are looking for in this time of chaos and fear. You tell us that Perfect Love (Jesus) casts out all fear. Give us courage and humility and a desire to give You our fear. When all around us is anger, hatred, panic, and isolation, help us to SEEK You and Your peace. When we turn to our country, our government, our finances, our spouse, or our friends in hopes that they will give us security, only to find anxiety and inner turmoil in their hold on us, remind us that those things are temporary and will never be able to meet our needs and desires. Only You can fulfill us. Only You give us rest during the storms of life. Only You are eternal. As we struggle to 'get ahead' and fight for 'our rights,' prick our souls with the reminder that You, our King, were a servant to the masses that You loved and that You gave up every right that was Yours. Take our gaze off this temporal world and let us focus on the Eternal Home You have prepared for us. As we live with the daily reminder that we are losing in this life…remind us, O God, that though we may lose for a time, in You we will win for eternity! Glory to our Savior, our Redeemer, our King! Amen.

Dawnita P., Drexel, MO

Dear Heavenly Father, Thank You for Your perfect love. May everyone who reads this devotional long to be in Your presence. May they abide in You and allow Your perfect love to transform how they think about themselves and others, transform what they say, and transform what they do. May the readers be so overwhelmed by Your love that they are able to die to themselves daily and walk in Your perfect will for their lives. Holy Spirit, guard their hearts and minds in Christ Jesus, so as they are reading about Your truth, they may recognize if they have believed any lies of the enemy. May the truth of Your love free them from any lies, and allow them to walk in the abundant life You have for each one of them. In the name of Jesus, Amen.

Katrina C., Los Patos, Dominican Republic

Lord, You said in Your word (Deuteronomy 31:8) that You will go before us, that You will be with us, that You will never fail us nor will You abandon us and that we need not be fearful nor be dismayed. Dear friend as you read, I pray that your faith is renewed and that your belief is restored in our Lord and Savior, Jesus Christ. I pray you will live fearlessly and trust God at his word, standing on His promise that He will never fail you. Rest assured my friend that you are never alone - I go boldly in prayer for you. It's in the never-failing name of Jesus Christ that I pray, Amen.

Charity R., Kansas City, MO

Heavenly Father, I pray every reader finds peace in You during their time spent reading this devotion. May they find not only peace, but understanding, knowledge, and guidance. May their hearts learn to reach You and may their desires for their life become Your desires for their life. In Jesus' name, Amen. Thank you.

Valencia G., Kansas City, MO

Father God, thank You that You are Love and that love is the motivation for all of Your interactions with us, including and especially Your self-revelation in Scripture. Your Word really is a "lamp unto [our] feet and a light unto [our] path" illuminating the darkness so we can see the way in which You would have us to go, and allowing us to see the beauty of who You are more clearly.

Father, I pray that the heart of each person reading this devotional is fertile ground for Your truth to land and take root. Whatever they may be dealing with, I pray that for these few minutes each day they will lay aside everything that would try to distract them from hearing what You desire to speak to them. Meet each person where they are and wrap Your loving arms around them as they commit this time to You, and I pray they will experience the gift of Your presence. May their love and desire for You grow with each turn of the page until they are convinced, without a shadow of a doubt, of the depth and magnitude of Your unfailing love for them. In the matchless name of Jesus the Christ, I pray, Amen!

Vernita A., Atlanta, GA

Father, thank You for the opportunity to be able to pray and encourage others, to "stand still and know that You are God" (Psalm 46:10). Today I encourage the reader to stay in the Word of God, for it is life to those who diligently seek Him.

Rebecca E., Kansas City, MO

For all the brothers, and all the sisters in Christ, I stretch out my hands to our heavenly Father, for all of you, to seal your well-being with our heavenly Father, and to ask a special blessing of love for your care and spiritual prosperity. "For this cause, since the day we met all of you Christians, we have not stopped praying for you, and asking God to fill you with the knowledge of His will through all spiritual wisdom and understanding. And we pray this in order that you may live a life worthy of the Lord and may please Him in every way" (Colossians 1:9–10). Amen

James E., Kansas City, MO

Dear Heavenly Father, thank you for the privilege to come to You in prayer on behalf of the readers of this devotional. Thank You Lord for the author and her heart for You and others. Lord, I ask that You bless each and every reader that we may know You not only as the God of our salvation but also as the God of our every waking moment. May we experience Your overwhelming presence each day of this life as we will in eternity. Lord, may we honor You with our thoughts, our words and our deeds. In the precious name of Jesus Christ, I pray this prayer. Amen.

Tracey R., Kansas City, MO

Dear Heavenly Father, I thank You for the love You have poured into these words. I pray that even before the reader gets to the last page that they have had an opportunity to witness the love contained within this text first hand; that they may know You or come to know You with greater depth. And in that knowledge Lord, I pray that it is more than surface, but that in every interaction they can know of Your love, not because they read the words, but because they felt Your Holy Spirit whispering to them as they read, that this Love is for them. I pray Father, that in each day they were able to tuck away a nugget that will be pinned to their heart and come to remembrance at a time that they need to be reminded of Your love, or that they need to share that love with the world. Father, I thank You that Your love is so great, so far, so wide, that it traveled from the author's heart to the readers heart, that they may know You through her. Father, I pray that just because they have finished the book, they will not stop seeking out Your love, but instead that they would develop a thirst so strong to be loved so much, that they will seek You out and share Your love with a piercing conviction. In Christ's name, Amen.

Jessica T., Kansas City, MO

Nevertheless He saved them for His name's sake, That He might make His mighty power known.

PSALMS 106:8

Chapter 1
PRESERVED BY LOVE

Learning outcomes for chapter 1:

- ✓ Understand that God never abandons the ones He loves
- ✓ See God's ultimate purpose of eternity with Him being worked out as He used ordinary men and women to achieve His purposes
- ✓ See God preserving the lineage that led to Jesus the Redeemer
- ✓ See God's love extended to everyone individually

Created with Love

In the beginning God created the heavens and the earth.

GENESIS 1:1

More than likely you've read the story of creation in the book of Genesis and thought of it as just that: a story about creation. Perhaps you viewed it as someone else's opinion of creation, or even thought of it as a myth about creation. If so, you missed not only the truth of creation, but you also missed the love story embedded in all that God created for us to enjoy. You missed the love that went into each act of creation: the sun, moon, stars, oceans, firmament, cattle and beasts – each one proclaimed by Him to be good. You didn't understand as you read the story of creation that God's 'good' is so much higher than anything we can imagine. Genesis tells us that on day six of creation, God created man, stepped back and surveyed the work of creation and proclaimed all that He had done to be 'very good' (Genesis 1:31).

I've often marveled at the many shades of green in creation. I believe that every wonder we see in nature could have been created just as beautifully by Him in shades of black, white and gray; we would not have known the difference. Instead, God created the rainbow in nature. I believe it was for His glory and for us to enjoy. His word says He knew each of us long before the foundations of the earth were laid. He knew you would like oceans and I would like mountains and someone else would revel in glaciers or deserts and the deep recesses of the ocean. His loving hand created the wonders of nature for us to enjoy. Even in its current sin-scarred shape we see wonders in His creations that cause us to catch our breath. In each creation we find the often-repeated beat of His heart:

"I will be their God, and they will be my people." He created beauty for the ones He loves.

Yet, despite the beauty of the creations around us, we long for Eden. We spend an earthly lifetime searching for what Adam and Eve lost. We look for utopia in the riches of this world, in endless philosophies and in failing man-made promises. Sometimes we catch glimpses of God's planned perfection: in the toes of a newborn, in the giggle and wiggle of a two-year-old, in the perfectly aligned stars on a moonlit night, or in the perfect sunrise or sunset. The promises of eternity and perfection are all around us, but we are rarely quiet long enough to hear the One who looks on and longs to whisper truth and love into our hearts.

Our longing for Eden is not our longing for the perfect creation, but for its Creator. We long for the only One who can fill the void that shadows our days. We long for the one who loved us so much He provided a way back to Him, in spite of our sin. We long to experience the perfect love that He alone offers. We unconsciously search for the perfect relationship that Adam and Eve had with God as they walked with Him each day in the garden. We seek it in every smile and every contact, but it is only found in Him.

Because of God's unfailing love, we will one day again have access to the tree of life, eternity, and perfection. We will have access to not just one, but many trees of life. Like Adam and Eve, before their sin, we will be in the presence of God and have the blessings of His presence and be able to enjoy all that He intended for us to experience in His original creation. Revelation 22:1–5 promises: "And he showed me a pure river of water of life, clear as crystal, proceeding from the throne of God and of the Lamb. In the middle of its street, and on either side of the river, was the tree of life, which bore twelve fruits, each tree yielding its fruit every month. The leaves of the tree were for the healing of the nations. And there shall be no more curse, but the throne of God and of the Lamb shall be in it, and His servants shall serve Him. They shall see His face, and His name shall be on their foreheads. There shall be no night there: They need no lamp nor light of the sun, for the Lord God gives them light. And they shall reign forever and ever."

Adam and Eve disobeyed God's instructions, and because of their sin we suffer the loss of the garden and all that it represented. But our God never fails; He didn't default on the love that He has for you and me as He created Eden. Knowing that we would need a Savior and hope for tomorrow, His love endures into eternity and brings the sure fulfillment of the promise that His love will never leave us. Rest in that hope today.

* * *

Time in His Word:

Read Genesis chapter 1

Prayer:

Father thank You for creation, for the many shades of green and all the colors of creation. Thank You for showing us who You are through Your creation. I look at creation and marvel, knowing Your omnipotence through Your design, and knowing that I've only scratched the surface of knowing who You are. And then Father, I remember that You also created me in Your image and I am humbled. Thank You for the reminders of Your presence in Your design. In the name of Jesus Christ. Amen.

Meditations and Journaling:

When you are quiet and honest, what do you long for? When you are quiet and honest, what are you most thankful for?

DAY 2

In the Garden

*And out of the ground the Lord God made every tree
grow that is pleasant to the sight and good for food.
The tree of life was also in the midst of the garden,
and the tree of the knowledge of good and evil.*

GENESIS 2:9

It started out good; perfect, even. Adam and Eve in the garden of Eden with God. Naming the animals, tending the garden, naked and unashamed. Walks with God in the cool of the day. Perfect unity with God, perfect peace with each other. Then, sin.

God placed Adam in the garden of Eden, a perfect paradise. In the garden were two important trees: the tree of life, and the tree of the knowledge of good and evil. In all that Adam and Eve were instructed to do, God's one prohibition was not to eat from the tree of the knowledge of good and evil. "And the Lord God commanded the man, saying, "Of every tree of the garden you may freely eat; but of the tree of the knowledge of good and evil you shall not eat, for in the day that you eat of it you shall surely die" (Genesis 2:16–17). In the midst of freedom and perfection, one prohibition, one thing not to do. Then the serpent who was "more cunning than any beast of the field which the Lord God had made" (Genesis 3:1), slithered into paradise, twisting the words of God, convincing Eve and then Adam to exercise their free will and make a choice contrary to God's truth. This is sin, when we choose to know more than the Creator and follow our own way.

After sin, everything changed. Adam and Eve went from innocence before each other and before God to shame, with a need to cover themselves and cower before God. The transformation was instant. The eyes of both Adam and Eve were opened; they were filled with false wisdom. There was shame and pride rising up to justify their disobedience. "The serpent deceived me," said Eve, intuitively recognizing deception and realizing its impact - after the fact. "The woman whom you gave to be with me, she gave me fruit of the tree, and I ate" (Genesis 3:12–14 ESV), said Adam, passing off the blame and conveniently overlooking his responsibility. This sin episode drove the first wedge in Adam and Eve's relationship. The serpent appeared to have made his first inroads into creating havoc and discrediting God.

There were consequences for their sin. First, the serpent: his promised destruction. For Eve: pain in childbirth and friction in the marriage relationship. For Adam: hard work until the day of his death. There it was, the end that God promised: death.

God said to Adam: "In the day you eat of it you will die" (Genesis 2:17). Because of their sin, death came in many ways. Their life instantly became a long slow progression toward that promised end. God cannot lie; they began to die with the first bite of the fruit. They began to see the fulfillment of God's pronouncement in so many ways. There was death of the perfection planned for mankind by God, the paradise in Eden. Now they faced physical death, a concept never imagined in their time in the garden. Most profound was the spiritual death reflected in their changed relationship with God. There were no more walks with Him in the cool of the evenings. There was also death of innocence, because now they knew pride, evil, cunning, and the consequences of sin.

So, where is the love story in shame, consequences, pride, and death?

The love story resides in the character of God. Never changing, He loved them on the day they sinned as much as on the day of their creation. He is God and because of His great love, He had already prepared a way back to Eden. He knew their response to the serpent in advance and He foreordained that mankind would not be lost to inherited sin and death. He prepared a way out of sin and back to Himself for Adam and Eve and their descendants. He divinely prescribed a way that will lead mankind back to sinless perfection and an endless relationship with Him.

God prepared a way back to Him for you, for me. He never intended for death to be your end. Despite what you may think, He has never stopped loving you. He opened His arms to you and maintains that gesture of openness all the days of your life. He is calling you back to Himself and providing a way that supersedes the pain of the consequences you call down upon yourself.

Always remember His open arms, waiting for you, despite your sin.

* * *

Time in His Word:

Read Genesis chapter 2

Prayer:

Father, help us to see your open arms and to hear your voice. Help our unbelief so that we do not spurn your perfect love in favor of lesser things. In the name of Jesus Christ. Amen.

Meditations and Journaling:

Have you sinned and assumed God has stopped loving you? You are here today, breathing and alive, because He loves you. Pause in your busyness to number the many ways that His love still surrounds you, in spite of your human frailty.

DAY 3
Evidence of Love

See what kind of love the Father has given to us, that
we should be called children of God; and so we are.

1 JOHN 3:1 ESV

Consequences of sin are not always immediate and not always immediately discernible to the person involved. Although we'd like to be able to calculate the end of the consequences of our sin, there is not usually a one-to-one ratio between sin and its consequences. Sometimes the consequences of our sin are far-reaching, extending late into our lives, and sometimes to other generations. Adam and Eve sinned and God made pronouncements about their consequences. Then, He announced their departure from the garden of Eden: "Therefore the Lord God sent him out of the garden of Eden to till the ground from which he was taken" (Genesis 3:23). These consequences for a bite of fruit seem harsh and severe, even unloving.

But look closer and see God's love. He cannot contradict Himself, even for those He loves. He has provided ways for His love to reach even into the recesses of perceived darkness. In the garden, in addition to the tree of the knowledge of good and evil, was a tree of life. God forbade them from eating of the tree of the knowledge of good and evil, but He did not forbid them from eating of the tree of life. However, they were not tempted by the tree of life. It had the power of eternal life. God put them out of the garden to keep them from being tempted to relieve their sentence of death by eating from the tree of life. More importantly, He put them out of the garden to prevent them from living forever in their current state of sin: "And now, lest he put out his hand and take also of the tree of life, and eat, and live forever" (Genesis 3:22). So, God forced them from the garden

OLIVIA DAVENPORT

and placed guards over the entrance, lest they scheme to re-enter. His love was hiding in plain sight as He decreed their removal and escorted them from the garden.

Before escorting them out of paradise, God sacrificed animals and replaced Adam and Eve's coverings of leaves. "And the Lord God made for Adam and for his wife garments of skins and clothed them" (Genesis 3:21 ESV). The covering they made for themselves was woefully inadequate for the life they were facing, so God prepared a covering for His children that would sustain them where they were going. This new covering was more than literal; it was a symbolic covering of His love and a foreshadowing of the blood sacrifice that would be made by Jesus to cover sins of the world. Love, indeed!

Preparing to administer discipline, parents often tell their children: "This hurts me more than it hurts you." Until they have children of their own, this saying makes no sense to them and they scoff at what we say. I believe our Parent God was immensely grieved over the sin of Adam and Eve and the long-term implications for all mankind. Our sin hurts His heart and He cannot fail to discipline us for our sin, but in love and with an eye toward our future reconciliation and perfection. We cover electrical outlets – He covered the entrance to the garden of Eden. We do our best to prepare our children for this world, but our best covering could never equal the covering provided when Jesus sacrificed His life for us on a wooden cross. He gave His highest for our best.

* * *

Time in His Word:

Read Genesis chapter 3

Prayer:

Father, forgive me for my sins, for grieving Your heart of love. Thank You for covering my sin with the blood of Your Son Jesus Christ, Immanuel, God with us. Help me Father, to see Your hand in my discipline and consequences and to understand Your heart of love in each action. In the name of Jesus Christ. Amen.

Meditations and Journaling:

Is there unconfessed sin in your life that you have allowed to linger? Handle that now, and know that even in the consequences God will always love you. Do not allow unconfessed sin to limit the freedom God desires you to experience in Him.

DAY 4
Real Life?

the son of Enos, the son of Seth, the
son of Adam, the son of God.

LUKE 3:38

As children, we spend a lot of time planning our lives and deciding what we will do once we are grown and 'out of the house,' away from the watchful eyes of our overprotective parents. We imagine the fun and freedom we will have once we are finally grown and on our own. Adam and Eve never had a reason for those rhetorical wanderings of the mind; no reason to wish themselves away from the garden and away from the love that surrounded them in their everyday relationship with the Father. Suddenly, there they were, thrust into what we would call 'real life.'

They were now in the school of hard knocks, in real life, experiencing tough love. They experienced the day-to-day grind of tilling the earth for food to eat, pain with childbirth, and only physical death to look forward to as life wore on. It was manifestly different from life in Eden. And, there were foreign emotions to deal with: anger, jealousy, lies and murder. The pain of one child murdering another, and the wandering away of the firstborn. These events and emotions were all foreign to Adam and Eve, and so different from the life they had before sin. This new life was the consequence of deception and the exercise of free will. Every temptation is an opportunity to choose to glorify God. They had instead chosen what seemed good to the eyes and the flesh and so there they were, out of Eden, living a life different than the life God planned for them.

It is easy to become mired in the story of hopelessness if we don't look for the details that signal God's love and promised hope for mankind. The story of Adam and Eve's first two sons, Cain and Abel, seemed to emphasize hopelessness. Cain became jealous of his brother's favor with God and killed him, the first murder recorded in scripture. The family now lived in a climate of jealousy, anger, lies and murder. God sentenced Cain to a life of separation – separation from God and from his family. He became a wanderer and a vagabond, looking over his shoulder for the blow that would kill him, except for the mark that God placed on him that protected him from that fate (Genesis 4:15). Adam and Eve essentially lost two sons – a parent's worst heart wound. Scripture says Adam lived 930 years (Genesis 5:5). We don't know his age when they left the garden; perhaps there was no reckoning of time at that point. But, imagine having more than 800 years to grieve and imagine what life would have been like if they had chosen not to eat that small bite of forbidden fruit.

"And Adam knew his wife again, and she bore a son and named him Seth, "For God has appointed another seed for me instead of Abel, whom Cain killed." And as for Seth, to him also a son was born; and he named him Enosh. Then men began to call on the name of the Lord"

(Genesis 4:25–26). Hope and promise for the future wrapped up in a small infant. A signal that one day mankind would once again call on the name of the Lord and experience a relationship with Him in a way that would wash away all the times of pain and hopelessness. Seth and Enosh are counted in the lineage of Jesus (Luke 3:38). God's love is never without a plan. The actions of mankind are never unaccounted for in God's plans.

Adam never stopped being the son of God (Luke 3:38). By his own choices, he removed himself from the immediate presence of God in the garden, but His Father never stopped loving him, never stopped coveting a relationship with him, never stopped caring for him. Even in the darkest of moments, God was there, caring for his child, and preparing a way back to paradise for all of mankind.

* * *

Time in His Word:

Read Genesis 4

OLIVIA DAVENPORT

Prayer:

Our Father in heaven, on bended knee and with repentant hearts, we plead with You - forgive us for breaking Your heart. Help us to see our sin and our distance from You. We repent Father and ask that You once again draw us close. We have forgotten our way home Father; show us how to draw close to You. Thank You for sharing Your word so we will always know that Your love is unconditional and never changes. Thank You Father. In the name of Jesus Christ. Amen.

Meditations and Journaling:

Is there something in your life that has removed you from the closeness of your relationship with God? Perhaps it is a relationship, another passion, or the unconscious seeking after the things of this world that draws you away. Remember that He has not moved away from you, instead you have moved away from Him. Start today to understand that His promises of love and forgiveness never expire and include anything you may have done. Begin to move closer to Him today. Tear down your wall of separation.

DAY 5
Cannonball

> *He who does not love does not know God, for*
> *God is love. In this the love of God was manifested*
> *toward us, that God has sent His only begotten Son*
> *into the world, that we might live through Him*

1 JOHN 4:8–9

Before Adam tasted the fruit offered by Eve, God had a plan in place that would cover our sin and redeem all mankind, reconciling us back to God. His words to the serpent spoke of the plan, a human offspring that would thwart the plans of Satan and bruise his head, killing the planned evil: "I will put enmity between you and the woman, and between your offspring and her offspring; he shall bruise your head, and you shall bruise his heel" (Genesis 3:15 ESV). The love of God called for the redemption of sinful mankind. The offspring of the woman, Jesus, would come and bruise the head of the serpent, killing his plans for the death, destruction and hopelessness of mankind. Each lesson in the Bible testifies about God's love for us, and heralds the coming of the promised Redeemer.

In the Old Testament, we see the lineage of the Redeemer Jesus to come, through the lines of Abraham, Isaac, Jacob and others. We see God protecting and preserving that lineage. As the human story unfolded, we see the hand of God, allowing our frailties and mindless decisions, but loving us back to eternity and offering His hand to guide us. His agape love will never stop seeking our highest good. Like a cannonball dive into a pool, His love splashes onto all the bystanders and leaves them dripping with gratitude.

Joseph, the favorite son of Jacob, was sold to Ishmaelite traders at age

OLIVIA DAVENPORT

seventeen by his brothers for twenty pieces of silver. The brothers lied to their father Jacob, saying that Joseph had been attacked and killed by wild animals. Jacob grieved, but God's love would not let the lie be true. His plan was unfolding in spite of the actions against Joseph that were meant for evil. As we understand more about Joseph's life, we see how God was actively preserving the offspring of Adam and Eve to bruise the head of the serpent.

The Ishmaelites traveled to Egypt where Joseph was again sold, this time to Potiphar, the captain of the guards for Pharaoh (Genesis 39:2). In God's unfolding plan, and because of the favor of God, Joseph became overseer in the house of Potiphar. When Potiphar's wife attempted to seduce Joseph, he refused and was thrown into prison because of her accusations. Once again Joseph was favored, this time by the keeper of the prison (Genesis 39:21). Later, when Pharaoh needed dreams interpreted and could find no one among his magicians and wise men to interpret the disturbing dreams, a former prisoner remembered Joseph, who had interpreted his dream while in prison. Pharaoh sent for Joseph and through God, Joseph was able to interpret the dreams of the Pharaoh (Genesis 41:16). Joseph was seen as wise and discerning by Pharaoh and soon became Pharaoh's second in command, over all of Egypt. "The Lord was with him; and whatever he did, the Lord made it prosper" (Genesis 39:23). Never forget that God sees all the events of your life as well and His favor is present in all your circumstances, even when times seem unfair.

In the passage of time, Joseph is reunited with his brothers when they came to Egypt to buy grain during the famine that devastated Canaan and Egypt. In their reunion we see the hand of the God of reconciliation, the heart of God for family, and the faithfulness of God in preserving His people for the coming of our Savior. Like waters from a cannonball the love of God in Joseph's heart overflowed as he is reconciled to his older brothers first, then his younger brother Benjamin, and finally his father Jacob. Seeing his father after more than twenty years, Joseph was overcome and "fell on his neck and wept on his neck a good while" (Genesis 46:29).

Joseph's brothers were guilty, ashamed and bracing for retribution. But the love that Joseph had experienced from God prepared him to offer them unconditional love, provisions, and protection from the famine for them and their families in Egypt. God's love overflowed the boundaries of Joseph's heart. He reassured his brothers, saying: "But now, do not therefore be grieved or angry with yourselves because you sold me here; for God sent me before you to preserve life" (Genesis 45:5). God is always looking beyond what we see with our natural eyes into the future eternity that He plans with His children.

Joseph could have felt like God dealt him a bad hand, but instead, he was able to see beyond his circumstances, viewing them in light of God's revealed purposes in his life. How about you? Are you dealing with something that seems unfair in your life? Joseph's strength came from his close relationship with God. In every circumstance he walked with God and let others see God in him. He chose not to be bitter. He chose to know God deeply. He chose to honor God with His life. He chose to see life through spiritual eyes. The love Joseph experienced in his walk with God overflowed onto everyone in his life, splashes of love and grace everywhere he went.

* * *

Time in His Word:

Read 1 Thessalonians 5:9–10, 16–22 and Hebrews 12:14–15

Prayer:

Lord, draw me close. I know that my choices matter. Help me to intentionally choose not to be bitter because of injustice in my life. In the name of Jesus Christ. Amen.

Meditations and Journaling:

How has your relationship with God changed because of your painful circumstances? Did you draw closer to Him in your circumstances, or did you move away?

With a Mighty Hand

*Israel saw the great power that the Lord used against
the Egyptians, so the people feared the Lord, and
they believed in the Lord and in his servant Moses.*

EXODUS 14:31 ESV

Moses was raised in the palace of Pharaoh as the adopted son of Pharaoh's daughter, with his biological mother as his nurse. As Moses grew older, he began to be interested and involved in the affairs of the people he was biologically related to. But he was not yet ready for the 'good works which God prepared beforehand' for him to do (Ephesians 2:10). God needed to prepare him for his part in preserving the seed destined to crush the head of the serpent. The lessons of scripture are a picture of God's consistent love for all mankind, shown through the ages as He allowed willing individuals to be a part of His redemption plan. Moses was a part of that plan.

Moses was educated in the finer things of Egypt and exposed to the things that would be valuable when he came back to ask Pharaoh to let the people of God go. The seventy Israelite people of Joseph's family who initially moved to Egypt during the famine had now grown into a nation. A new Pharaoh ruled in place of the Pharaoh who knew Joseph and allowed Joseph's family to live peacefully in the land of Egypt. This new ruler governed them with a harsh hand, fearful because of their numbers and fearful that they might turn against him if there was ever a conflict with another nation (Exodus 1:8–10). As a young man, Moses observed the continual mistreatment of his people. Intervening in a dispute involving one of his countrymen, Moses impetuously killed an Egyptian and buried his body in a shallow grave. This led to Pharaoh hunting Moses to kill him. Moses had to run for his life (Exodus 2:11–15). He fled to Midian where he lived for forty years, getting married and having two sons before God called to him from a burning bush and commissioned him to lead the Israelites out of Egypt.

"Then the children of Israel groaned because of the bondage, and they cried out; and their cry came up to God because of the bondage" (Exodus 2:23). Moses returned to Egypt, having been forewarned by God that the Pharaoh would not let the people go easily (Exodus 4:21). God called the people of Israel His 'firstborn' (Exodus 4:22). God is striding into Pharaoh's camp as a mighty warrior coming to redeem his children. Moses is His instrument, called to lead God's people from their oppressor, first making a simple request which was later followed with plagues that devastated the nation. After nine plagues, Pharaoh is nearly depleted, but still battling to maintain ownership and supremacy over God's people, refusing to let his slave forces leave the land where they are now held captive. God announces to Moses the last plague that would force Pharaoh to let the people go. In fact, Pharaoh would angrily drive them out of the land. "The Lord said to Moses, "Yet one plague more I will bring upon Pharaoh and upon Egypt. Afterward he will let you go from here. When he lets you go, he will drive you away completely" (Exodus 11:1 ESV).

The tenth plague announced by God, the death of all the unprotected firstborn in the land of Egypt - both man and beast, caused Pharaoh to drive the Israelites from Egypt. To protect the Israelite nation from the death that was coming, God instituted the Passover, calling for the Israelites to slaughter a lamb and put some of the blood of the lamb on the doorposts of their homes. The blood placed on the doorposts and the lintels of the Israelite homes caused the angel of death to 'pass over' the Israelite houses on the night of the tenth plague: "that you may know that the Lord does make a difference between the Egyptians and Israel" (Exodus 11:7). The Passover instituted to prepare for this plague was spiritually significant to the nation of Israel for all of its history, even unto today. After the tenth plague, Pharaoh was defeated; the gods of Egypt were defeated. The Lord Jehovah announced His supremacy with a mighty hand. He rescued His firstborn from the oppressor, foreshadowing the rescue of people who choose Him from the hand of Satan.

God has not changed. He will also rescue you: today, now, for eternity.

OLIVIA DAVENPORT

He will deliver you from the hand of the enemy and from your situation. The Lord makes a difference for eternity between those who are the children of faith and those who spurn His Son Jesus. The Passover blood was symbolic of the blood shed by Jesus at Calvary. When you choose Christ Jesus as your Lord and Savior, you are symbolically covered by the blood of Jesus and you are clothed in His righteousness. When God looks at you, He sees the righteousness of Jesus instead of your sin. The penalty due for your sin (death) will be replaced by the grace of God. The sentence of eternal death and separation from God will 'pass over' you.

Jesus said "I am the way, the truth and the life" (John 14:6). His blood is your instrument of rescue. Seek Him today.

* * *

Time in His Word:

Read Psalm 77:15–20; Romans 5:8; 2 Corinthians 5:21; Hebrews 11:24–29

Prayer:

Thank You Jesus, the King and the Lamb, for providing Your blood to cleanse me from all unrighteousness for all of eternity. In the name of Jesus Christ. Amen.

Meditations and Journaling:

What situation are you facing now that you need deliverance from? Do you believe God can rescue you? Has He come to your rescue in the past? Ask Him for deliverance now.

DAY 7
Fathers and Sons

In your seed all the nations of the earth shall be
blessed, because you have obeyed My voice."

GENESIS 22:18

When expecting a daughter, men are often told that 'she will have you wrapped around her little finger in no time at all.' This is mostly true - fathers quickly fall prey to the wiles of their daughters. However, the father/ son relationship is just as pivotal, but in a different way. The bond that father and son have cannot be replicated in any other relationship. Sons may grow up to have relationships with other men, but fathers who are active in the lives of their sons leave an indelible handprint that cannot be erased and have lasting impact. Scripture shows us several father/son relationships, relationships that were sometimes flawed, but showed the deep impact that relationship had on the father and on the son, and on their legacy for generations. We see the love between Abraham and Isaac, Isaac and Esau, Jacob and Joseph, and most importantly, Jesus and His Father. Scripture shows us a recurring theme of deliverance in these father/ son relationships.

In their old age, Abraham aged 100, and Sarah aged 90 (Genesis 17:17), were blessed by God with a child. " And Abraham called the name of his son who was born to him--whom Sarah bore to him—Isaac" (Genesis 21:3). The name Isaac means laughter, reflecting their joy in this blessing of a child from the loins of Abraham to the barren womb of Sarah. Abraham made a great feast on the day Isaac was weaned. Isaac was the fulfillment of a promise from God and the heir promised to Abraham that would continue Abraham's lineage and become a great nation. But God tested Abraham. Abraham, even in his joyful state, needed to love and reverence God more than this promised child.

When God came to Abraham and told him to sacrifice his son, his son of promise, Abraham obediently made preparations. He did not question God. He took Isaac, a few servants, wood, fire and rope to the mountain that God directed him to. Abraham trusted that God would remain true to His covenant promise – the promise that said Isaac was the promised heir from whom nations of faith would grow. Abraham didn't ask to know how God would make this happen, but had faith that He would. On the basis of that faith, he was willing to sacrifice his son Isaac. When he arrived at the mountain, he prepared the wood for sacrifice, bound Isaac and placed him on the altar and raised his knife to kill him. God stopped him at that moment: "And He said, "Do not lay your hand on the lad, or do anything to him; for now I know that you fear God, since you have not withheld your son, your only son, from Me" (Genesis 22:12). God provided a ram to sacrifice in the place of Isaac that day. There was worship on the mountain that day.

Generations later, in another Father / Son relationship, God sent His son Jesus to be sacrificed on a mountain. To the uninformed, it looked like the Jewish hierarchy had succeeded in silencing the voice that brought truth. But on a miraculous Sunday morning God raised His Son to life. This time there was need for death, for blood to be shed by the One who was the fulfillment of the lineage that God protected from Seth to Jesus. The Father loved the Son. The Son loved His Father. That love translated to obedience in giving His life. His blood was not shed in vain, but for the redemption of all mankind. God has not withheld His Son - His only Son, from us, for our deliverance.

Abraham renamed the mountain where he went to sacrifice Isaac. "Abraham called the name of the place, The-Lord-Will-Provide; as it is said to this day, "In the Mount of The Lord it shall be provided" (Genesis 22:14). Surely, for all mankind, God continues to provide.

* * *

Time in His Word:

Read Genesis 22

Prayer:

Thank you, Father for always providing. We do not know our deepest needs, yet You always meet us and provide for Your children. Our humble thanks are insufficient for all that You do for us, so we offer You our hearts in thanksgiving and rejoicing. In the name of Jesus, who provided what we didn't know we needed. Amen.

Meditations and Journaling:

Write about memories you have of your earthly father, or your memories of your life without him if that is the case. Examine how your relationship with your earthly father, or lack of a relationship, affects how you respond to our heavenly Father.

Stranger in Your Midst

For the Lord your God is God of gods and Lord of lords, the great God, mighty and awesome, who shows no partiality nor takes a bribe. He administers justice for the fatherless and the widow, and loves the stranger, giving him food and clothing.

DEUTERONOMY 10:17-18

No one is excluded. In God's economy, all are welcome and invited. We are all His children; there are no step-children, no grandchildren. We were all created in His image. His desire is that all His children know and love Him and love each other. He desires that we love as He does, caring for the widow, the orphan, and the stranger in our midst. For many people, their first glimpse of His love comes from those who have allowed His love to penetrate their hearts and show up in their actions. That is why we are commanded to love one another, to invite the stranger in and show him God's love.

The Israelites left Egypt under the mighty hand of God and settled in a new land. There were strangers around them and in their midst. God gave specific laws for how to treat those non-Israelites who chose to live inside the camp of the Israelites and those who were neighbors. Unequivocally, His desire was for those strangers to know Him, the God of the Israelite nation. The surest way to knowing Him was through His people and experiencing His love through them. God said to the Israelite nation: "The stranger who dwells among you shall be to you as one born among you, and you shall love him as yourself; for you were strangers in the land of Egypt: I am the Lord your God " (Leviticus 19:34). They were never to treat others as they had been treated in Egypt.

The stranger among the Israelites was only prohibited from participating in those rituals and observances that were dependent upon faith in the God of the Israelites. But their lack of knowledge and faith did not prevent them from being treated with the love God has for all His children. And, upon their choice to be united in faith, "he shall be as a native of the land" (Exodus 12:48–49).

God's love in the heart of a believer, extended to all without partiality, results in others coming to know Him. Unselfish love has the power to transform people, to cause their hearts to open like a rosebud coming into full bloom. Sharing His love with others invites them into His kindness, His mercy and His kingdom. What a great gift you are able to give someone just by loving them as you are loved by God. Many years after these laws were given to the Israelite nation, Jesus said: "'You shall love the Lord your God with all your heart, with all your soul, and with all your mind.' This is the first and great commandment. And the second is like it: 'You shall love your neighbor as yourself'" (Matthew 22:37–39).

We are made to give and receive love, but life tamps us down and soon we start responding in non-loving ways. Unlike our maker, we begin to dole out love in small doses to specific people for small spaces of time. Soon, we find we are unable to receive love and our ability to give love grows even smaller. We grieve through epidemics of loneliness and aloneness never intended by the Father when He created us. Letting His love fill and overflow to others is the only solution to the emptiness that occurs when life becomes too much.

* * *

Time in His Word:

Read Deuteronomy 10:17–19; Isaiah 56:1–8; Matthew 5:44–45

Prayer:

Heavenly Father, help me to remember the priority of love. Help me to know that the greatest thing I can cultivate is love, loving You first with all my heart, mind and soul. Help me to love my neighbor, the strangers I meet and all those You place in my life. May I always remember that love will never end and will never fail. You are love Father, guide me in Your ways. In the name of Jesus Christ. Amen.

Meditations and Journaling:

Allow yourself to remember when it was not hard to love others-a time before someone hurt you and you began to shut down. Are you allowing the love of God to fill you and overflow? Are you experiencing His love every day? How are you doing at loving the stranger in your midst, the fatherless, the widow? Write about a time when you were privileged to see love transform someone.

The Moabite Woman

Salmon begot Boaz by Rahab, Boaz begot
Obed by Ruth, Obed begot Jesse,

MATTHEW 1:5

God's relentless passion to redeem mankind back to Himself and a perfect state has never wavered. His promise of death to the serpent in Genesis 3:15 "…He shall bruise your head" pours out in the pages of scripture as willing men and women submitted to His will during their lifetimes and became ancestors to the promised Redeemer.

Like Joseph and his clan, Elimelech, his wife Naomi, and their two sons fled their home to find food during a famine. They landed in Moab, a country that was an enemy of Israel. The sons took wives from among the Moabite people. In the course of time, Elimelech and his two sons died. Naomi decided to return home to Bethlehem, Judah. She was bitter about life and her situation. She encouraged her daughters-in-law to return to their Moabite families. One daughter-in-law, Orpah, kissed her good-bye and left. Ruth, the other daughter-in-law, refuses to leave her. She clings to her mother-in-law, professing her loyalty and her faith. "For wherever you go, I will go; And wherever you lodge, I will lodge; Your people shall be my people, And your God, my God" (Ruth 1:16). Ruth, a woman from a tribe of foreign people and gods, had experienced the love and kindness of strangers and had come to know and love their God.

Naomi and Ruth traveled back to Bethlehem, Judah. Ruth immediately set out to take care of Naomi. In her care for Naomi, she was noticed by others as a foreigner and for her kindness and virtue. She worked in the fields of Boaz, an older man and near relative of Elimelech, who noticed her and offered many kindnesses to her through his workmen. She was favored as she worked in the fields of Boaz. Boaz's words to Ruth when she came to work in his fields providentially foretold the plans of the Lord and acknowledged her faith when he said: "The Lord repay your work, and a full reward be given you by the Lord God of Israel, under whose wings you have come for refuge" (Ruth 2:12).

In time, Boaz chose to fulfill the duties of a kinsman-Redeemer, marrying Ruth to preserve the lineage and heritage of Elimelech. When their son Obed was born, Ruth laid him in the arms of Naomi, who became his nurse (Ruth 4:16). Obed became the father of Jesse, who became the father of King David. God's covenant with David continued the line through which Jesus the Redeemer would come. Speaking of this lineage, God spoke to David through Nathan the prophet: "And your house and your kingdom shall be established forever before you. Your throne shall be established forever" (2 Samuel 7:16).

God is always seeking your highest good. We look back and see His hand in all things. He is never sleeping, unaware of you and what is going on in your life. In the bigger picture we see history steadily marching toward His planned redemption through Jesus Christ. In the nearer picture, we see His hand active in our lives, loving us, protecting us, molding us, drawing us closer and closer into intimate relationship with Him. The Redeemer came for us through the kindness of strangers based on the love of God.

* * *

Time in His Word:
Read Ruth chapter 4

Prayer:
Lord Jehovah, we have come under Your wings for refuge. Thank You for covering us, for protecting us, for loving us, for reminding us daily that we belong to You and that You will never leave us or forsake us. We thank You each day for your planned redemption and for reconciling us back to You. In the name of Jesus Christ. Amen.

Meditations and Journaling:
Where are you seeing the love of God in your life today?

DAY 10
Just One

Even so it is not the will of your Father who is in
heaven that one of these little ones should perish.

MATTHEW 18:14

You are individually important to God. We tend to read scripture and understand redemption for all men collectively, but we each need to see it personally. Redemption for you, just as you are. God's love covers YOU. The principle of each person being important is repeated in scripture and should be taken into your heart. YOU are important to God, just as you are.

God's character has many facets. He loves us individually. He shows us mercy and grace each day. He is holy and desires for His children to live without sin. And, He is righteous and just. He will never overlook sin because it offends His holiness and His righteousness. But even as He responds in justice to our life situations, we see His hand of mercy and grace.

God made a covenant with Abraham to bless all the nations of the earth through him, bringing the promised Messiah through the lineage of Abraham. Having reiterated this covenant with Abraham in Genesis chapter 18, God turned His face toward the sins of Sodom and Gomorrah. But He did not hide from Abraham the impending judgment. "The Lord said, "Shall I hide from Abraham what I am about to do, seeing that Abraham shall surely become a great and mighty nation, and all the nations of the earth shall be blessed in him? For I have chosen him, that he may command his children and his household after him to keep the way of the Lord by doing righteousness and justice, so that the Lord may bring to Abraham what he has promised him" (Genesis 18:17–19 ESV).

OLIVIA DAVENPORT

As God turned toward Sodom and Gomorrah in judgment, Abraham seized the opportunity to intercede for those living in Sodom who were righteous. "And Abraham came near and said, "Would You also destroy the righteous with the wicked?" (Genesis 18:23). Abraham stood before the Lord and pleaded for the righteous, asking the Lord to spare the place for the sake of the fifty righteous who might live there. "And the Lord said, "If I find at Sodom fifty righteous in the city, I will spare the whole place for their sake" Genesis 18:26 ESV). Abraham pressed further, pleading for the 40, 30, 20 and even the 10 righteous ones who might live there. God's heart of mercy agreed to spare the city for even ten righteous who might live there.

Years later, Jesus our Shepherd, came for even the one who would receive Him. In a parable, He emphasized the joy of finding that one out of a hundred who had gone astray (Luke 15:4–7). The one is important. You are important. When you accept your importance to Him, it changes your outlook and perspective; changes how you walk each day. ONE is important. YOU are important. "There will be more joy in heaven over one sinner who repents than over ninety-nine just persons who need no repentance" (Luke 15:7). God is still extending mercy today on an individual basis.

* * *

Time in His Word:

Read Genesis chapter 18; Psalm 56:8; Luke 12:6–7;

Prayer:

Lord, because of Your mercy I am chosen. I am just one, but You have chosen me to be a part of Your family. I was a stranger, but Your love cleansed me and brought me under your covering. Thank You Father that this one is now Your own. In the name of Jesus Christ. Amen.

Meditations and Journaling:

God knows your name. He is more than your Maker; He is the lover of your soul. You are precious to Him. Describe how that knowledge impacts you today, in this moment. What questions does it bring to mind? Bring those questions to Him. Wait in quiet expectation for His answer and revelations.

I have loved you with an everlasting love; therefore I have continued my faithfulness to you.

JEREMIAH 31:3 ESV

Chapter 2
THE CHARACTER OF LOVE

Learning outcomes for chapter 2 (Days 11-20)

- ✓ Understand that God's character of love includes mercy and compassion, but does not exclude justice
- ✓ God will not overlook sin even though He loves the sinner
- ✓ Our praise must be because of who God is, not because of what He does for us
- ✓ In His sovereignty, God may allow hard circumstances in the lives of His children, but He never withdraws His presence

Mercy and Justice

But the men of Sodom were exceedingly wicked and sinful against the Lord.

GENESIS 13:13

God will extend mercy; God will also chastise and destroy wickedness. His destruction is always prompted by the evil intentions and actions of man. In the days of Noah, God saw that every intention of the heart of man was evil always. His justice demanded an end to this serpent-induced climate of evil. It is important to know that God's character is love, and that His love includes correction, always moving us toward righteousness. God's justice is about administering deserved punishment or rewards based on our response to His standards.

Even in His justice toward wickedness, God is merciful. Mercifulness is His character. He will remove His righteous people before destruction. Despite Noah warning the people of his time about God's coming judgment, only Noah and his family were protected in the ark as destruction rained on the earth. When God approached Sodom, He saw Lot, his wife and two daughters living in a climate of immorality. God brought them out and then He brought destruction. "And it came to pass, when God destroyed the cities of the plain, that God remembered Abraham, and sent Lot out of the midst of the overthrow, when He overthrew the cities in which Lot had dwelt" (Genesis 19:29). This destruction of the people in Noah's time and on Sodom and the cities of the plain was God's justice for those who chose to live without acknowledging Him.

God will never destroy the righteous with the wicked. The judge of all the earth will always do right (Genesis 18:23–25). His chastisement is upon those who choose their own way over the ways of the One who created all things. Choosing Him does not mean you have reached perfection; it means you have acknowledged Him and His ways as right, and chosen to live according to His righteousness. This is the starting point. This is the place where we begin to understand love. God is more interested in mercy than punishment. He sent His prophet Jonah to Nineveh to tell a wicked nation about His mercy. He is zealous about a relationship with you and is patient with how we use our free will, allowing us time to know Him.

God created a perfect world for mankind. Adam and Eve chose a path that led all mankind into a life different than the perfection God planned. Their actions did not surprise Him. In His love, mercy and compassion, God provided a way back to Him through the death of His Son Jesus Christ. On a cross at Calvary Jesus poured out His life as a perfect sacrifice, opening the door for everyone to be reconciled to God and receive the promise of eternal life and perfection. The fulfillment of that promise requires a choice.

Like Adam and Eve, you must choose between obeying the voice of God or living in the consequences of not having Him in your life. Accepting Jesus as your Lord and Savior means you have chosen the complete character of God, receiving His hand of justice as well as His mercy for your life. Jesus opened the path to reconciliation to God; He is the only path to God's mercy. He said "I am the way, the truth and the life. No one comes to the Father except through me" (John 14:6).

It seems simple, but many do not choose God. Their choice results in God's judgment instead of His mercy. He will allow circumstances in your life that point you to Him; He will seek to win you over. He wants to bless you with perfection, eternal life and a relationship with Him, but the choice is yours; He will never force you to choose Him.

* * *

Time in His Word:

Read Isaiah 30:1, 18–21; 2 Peter 2:1–9

Prayer:

Our Father in heaven, thank you for the mercy you extend to us each day. Your mercies are new each morning. I acknowledge Your holiness and justice and thank You for opening the veil, allowing all those in who choose You through Your Son Jesus Christ. I choose the free gift of salvation offered by Jesus Christ's death on a cross at Calvary, and commit my life to You today. Thank You Father for the opportunity to show and tell others about You by my words and my life. In the name of Jesus Christ. Amen.

Meditations and Journaling:

Write about a recent example of God's mercy in your life. Where have you seen His justice? Each day pay attention to the examples of mercy and justice in your life. Tune in and seek to understand these aspects of His character, mercy and justice.

I Will Rescue You

You will not need to fight in this battle. Position yourselves, stand still and see the salvation of the Lord, who is with you, O Judah and Jerusalem!' Do not fear or be dismayed; tomorrow go out against them, for the Lord is with you."

2 CHRONICLES 20:17

Many people view Christianity as a passive religion, observed by a group of people mindlessly following the words of a centuries-old book that has no modern-day relevance. But the God of Christianity is by no means passive, weak or irrelevant. He delivers with a strong arm, requiring only our humble request to Him, believing that He is able to deliver us from any calamity that seeks to get in the way of His glory. As a loving parent, He rescues His children when they call. The Old Testament records many instances of God's deliverance. Second Chronicles chapters 14–21 record the many battles of Kings Asa and Jehoshaphat. Several lessons stand out from the lives of Kings Asa and Jehoshaphat that we need to remember as we expectantly wait for God to deliver us from our trials.

The Lord will fight your battles when you first submit yourself to Him, and then submit your cause to Him. King Jehoshaphat faced threats from the kings of nations surrounding him. 2 Chronicles 20:3 says he was afraid. However, it tells us that his first response was to *"seek the LORD."* He sought the LORD in faith, believing the word of the LORD and the power of the LORD to rescue the nation. This came from a lifetime of believing in the power of God and seeing the reality of God rescuing him time after time. Jehoshaphat stood before the house of the Lord and confidently proclaimed God's deliverance in advance: 'If disaster comes upon us, the sword, judgment, or pestilence, or famine, we will stand before this house and before you— for your name is in this house—and cry out to you in our affliction, and you will hear and save' (2 Chronicles 20:9 ESV). He knew His heavenly Father would save Him.

The Lord will fight your battles knowing that you are not perfect and that you will mess up. Like a loving parent, God already knows we will make wrong decisions, but that does not stop His love or His deliverance. King Jehoshaphat engaged in battle allied with King Ahab, a battle God's prophet warned against. King Ahab died in that battle. After God delivered Jehoshaphat safely from the battle, God's prophet spoke to him, saying: "Should you help the wicked and love those who hate the Lord? Therefore the wrath of the Lord is upon you. Nevertheless good things are found in you, in that you have removed the wooden images from the land, and have prepared your heart to seek God" (2 Chronicles 19:2–3). God does not overlook our blunders, but neither does He forget those whose hearts belong to Him.

King Asa began his reign over Judah restoring the people to faith in God, removing the idols in the land. Scripture records many years of peace under his leadership and victory in battle. However, in Asa's later years, he found himself relying on military might and alliances with other kings rather than trusting God and remembering the many times God had delivered him. Because of this foolishness, King Asa's last years were filled with unrest and there were many wars. When God's children choose to rely on self, God allows our detour and the resulting consequences, but He does not leave us.

Over and over scripture records that Kings Asa and Jehoshaphat 'had rest all around them' when they submitted themselves and their battles to God, trusting Him for rescue and deliverance. Like God did for Jehoshaphat and Asa, the Lord will fight your battles and there will be rest all around you when you submit your 'stuff' to Him. Yes, we will still experience battles, but as those battles are submitted to God, we will experience rest in the midst of those battles and the peace that surpasses understanding as we are assured that He takes care of His children.

Many people turn from God when they petition Him for rescue and then fail to see immediate, favorable, miraculous changes in their circumstances. They turn from Him when they fail to see exactly the

OLIVIA DAVENPORT

response they expected. They miss the point of His love, failing to understand that even when He rescues us, He has a purpose aimed for His glory. His rescue may not always be dramatic, (sometimes it is), but it will always teach us, grow our faith and draw us closer to Him. His rescue will always reinforce His promise to always be with us. His rescue will always bring us peace and hope in our circumstances. His rescue will always reinforce His plan and purpose for our lives. His rescue will always remind us of the fragility of life on this earth and the strength of His promise of eternity.

God's character does not change. He rescues His children even today. We must believe in His power to deliver us, act on that belief, and confidently proclaim His power to rescue us from any situation. We must remember that His agape love will always seek our highest good and that He will fight our physical battles as well as our spiritual battles. We must remember that He knows our frame, that we are dust (Psalm 103:14). He will rescue His children even when we make wrong decisions. He understands our imperfections, knows us perfectly and completely and still loves us.

* * *

Time in His Word:

Read Exodus 14:14; 2 Chronicles 20:15; Ephesians 6:11

Prayer:

Abba Father, time after time you come for us. Your mighty right hand saves us from ourselves, from our battles and from the situations we place ourselves into. Thank You. Our words are inadequate, but we honor You and trust You and revere You. You are our Father who loves us in spite of who we are, but also because of who we are. We are Yours Father and we submit every day to You. In the name of Jesus Christ. Amen.

Meditations and Journaling:

When were you rescued last? Think about the circumstances of your situation and remember how God saved you. Thank Him in prayer. Know that He is always there for you.

DAY 13
Covenantal Love

Then Jonathan made a covenant with David,
because he loved him as his own soul.

1 SAMUEL 18:3 ESV

God's agape love means that He is always seeking our highest good. His love for us allows circumstances in our lives that will draw us closer to Him. We may not always be able to see His highest good in our circumstances, but as we grow closer in relationship to Him, our history with Him will allow us to trust that His love will never lead us away from what is best for us. As we live in His love, we will heal and grow to be able to share that love with others and be blessed to experience that sacrificial covenantal love from others.

Scripture records the friendship of David and Jonathan, giving a glimpse of this sacrificial covenantal love. Scripture tells us that Jonathan loved David as his own soul. They made a covenant that would bind them together always, knitting their souls together. To symbolize this covenant, "Jonathan took off the robe that was on him and gave it to David, with his armor, even to his sword and his bow and his belt" (1 Samuel 18:4). This reminds me of promises made as kids, swapping a splotch of blood with a friend and swearing to always be blood brothers (or sisters). But, for Jonathan and David, this covenant meant real sacrifices and promises kept into the next generation. Rarely do we find friendship so genuine, lasting and sacrificial.

Jonathan was the son of King Saul, the first king of Israel. Under other circumstances Jonathan would be in line for the throne, but David had been anointed by Samuel the prophet as the one who would succeed Saul.

This alone could have been cause for bitter contention between David and Jonathan, but it was not. King Saul, however, because of jealousy, alternated between loving David and wanting to kill him. As his anger and jealousy grew, he sought the life of David. Jonathan, the confidant of his father, used his influence to keep David safe, finally sending David away from the presence of Saul to preserve his life. Before David left, Jonathan, acknowledging God's will for David to be king, asked David to promise protection for himself and his descendants "If I am still alive, show me the steadfast love of the Lord, that I may not die; and do not cut off your steadfast love from my house forever, when the Lord cuts off every one of the enemies of David from the face of the earth" (1 Samuel 20:14–15 ESV).

David left the palace and spent years in exile, hiding from King Saul. Nothing more is recorded of any interaction between David and Jonathan. Jonathan and King Saul died in battle and David ascended to the throne. After a time of war there was peace all around David. He remembered his covenant with Jonathan and asked "Is there still anyone who is left of the house of Saul, that I may show him kindness for Jonathan's sake?" (2 Samuel 9:1). By the providence of God there was a son of Jonathan still living. His name was Mephibosheth. David showed graciousness to Mephibosheth for the sake of his father Jonathan. So David said to him, "Do not fear, for I will surely show you kindness for Jonathan your father's sake, and will restore to you all the land of Saul your grandfather; and you shall eat bread at my table continually" (2 Samuel 9:7).

The covenantal love between Jonathan and David had far-reaching implications, even to the preservation of many generations of the house of King Saul. That is the nature of God's love. In our lives, the love we unashamedly extend to others reaches into places we could never imagine. That is the intent of God's love. Love your neighbor. Let God's love do its work in the hidden places of the heart of others, reaching in and rooting out hatred and division, creating actions that will extend into the next generation. God's love overlooks ailments. It did not matter to David that Mephibosheth was crippled. Agape love does not look at the outer man, but looks inside to the shriveled heart that needs the healing made possible only by the love of God, given freely.

* * *

Time in His Word:

Read 1 Samuel 18:1–4; 19:1–7; 20:1–41

Prayer:

Our Father, thank You for the example of Your love. Open my heart that I might receive all that You have for me. Open my heart that Your love will flow from me to others. Let me be Your vessel, pouring out to others. Teach me to seek the highest good of others. Allow me to see others as You see them and to seek to bandage the wounds that this life inflicts. Oh Father, teach me to love like You love. In the name of Jesus, who loved us with Your love and gave His life for each one of us. Amen.

Meditations and Journaling:

Who do you love unashamedly and without reservation? In what ways are you continually seeking their highest good? In your circle of family and friends, who loves you unreservedly, fully, completely and seeks your highest good? In what ways are you preventing others from loving you completely? Think of one thing you can do that would allow others to love you more.

DAY 14
Sovereign and Merciful

(For the Lord is our Judge, The Lord is our Lawgiver;
The Lord is our King; He will save us);

ISAIAH 33:22

I sat before the casket and grieved. I remembered the days past, the smiles, the hugs, the meals, the fellowship. I watched the young man try to stem the flow of tears as he remembered all that his grandfather had meant to him, the times they shared. Now, those days were over, no more to be. And You, Father, reminded me in my grief that this life is not all there is. In my grief You gave me hope. You reminded me that You are merciful, that Your ways are not my ways; Your thoughts are higher than my thoughts. You gave me the hope that I badly needed as I mourned. You reminded me of Your provision.

David mourned the child he had with Bathsheba. This child, a product of adultery, resulting in the murder of Bathsheba's prior husband Uriah, was struck by God and died seven days after birth. David's sins were deserving of death. Mercifully, God forgave David, but the consequences allowed by the Sovereign God would ever remind David of his sins. David's actions had profaned the name of God for all to see. Nathan the prophet proclaimed God's punishment for David's sins: "So David said to Nathan, "I have sinned against the Lord." And Nathan said to David, "The Lord also has put away your sin; you shall not die. However, because by this deed you have given great occasion to the enemies of the Lord to blaspheme, the child also who is born to you shall surely die" (2 Samuel 12:13–14). The Sovereign God chose to be merciful to David. This merciful encounter may have been what David recalled as he wrote Psalm 145:8, "The Lord is gracious and full of compassion, Slow to anger and great in mercy."

While the child lived, David lay all night on the ground, fasted and pleaded with God for the life of the child. After the child died, David got up, washed and anointed himself and went into the house of the Lord and worshipped. David expressed his actions this way: "While the child was alive, I fasted and wept; for I said, 'Who can tell whether the Lord will be gracious to me, that the child may live?' But now he is dead; why should I fast? Can I bring him back again? I shall go to him, but he shall not return to me" (2 Samuel 12:22–23). Even in his grief, David was reminded of the promises of eternity; he would see his child again.

Death and harsh circumstances of life come to us all. In our darkest hours, it seems that God does not hear, does not see our sorrow. It feels like there is no hope. David derived his hope from intimately knowing the God who holds the circumstances of our lives in His hands. David knew the God who had the power to give life or withhold life. David trusted God. In His grief, he went into the house of the Lord and worshipped. David knew the end: "I shall go to him, but he shall not return to me." This is the hope we have as we sit before the casket. God knows, God sees, His eyes are not shut to our sorrow. He has not stopped loving you. He is still worthy of worship, and He still sits on His throne. His ways are higher than our ways.

Circumstances tell us that God does not care, that He has not listened to our pleas, but circumstances lie. The sovereign God who decreed death at the first bite of the fruit, "You shall surely die," had already prepared a way back to perfection, back to Him. He decreed that one day we would never have to sit before a casket again. Sovereign and merciful, He ordained the seed that would redeem us and carefully nurtured the lineage of that seed throughout history so we could never doubt His everlasting love for all of mankind. Even as David sinned and suffered the consequences of that sin, God remembered His covenantal promise that the Savior would come through the line of David (2 Samuel 7:16). In due time Jesus came, clothed in humanity to proclaim the sovereignty of His Father in heaven and to demonstrate His mercy on the cross. Never forget His love. Never forget His sovereignty or His mercy.

* * *

OLIVIA DAVENPORT

Time in His Word:

Read Habakkuk 2:14; Ezekiel 36:22–28; Romans 9:20–24

Prayer:

LORD, we honor You. Help us to see Your hand in our lives. Help us to never forget that You are God and that You are deserving of honor and glory and that Your name is holy. Help us to proclaim the holiness of Your name everywhere we go. Let our lives bring You glory among the nations. And, let us always be thankful for the mercy You alone bestow on us, each day, every hour. In the name of Jesus Christ. Amen.

Meditations and Journaling:

Is it hard for you to accept the sovereignty of God? Did David's punishment seem harsh? Are there times when it seems God could have done things differently? Meditate on Romans 9:20–24 and ponder your response to His sovereignty. Shall we accept the mercy but not the sovereignty of our God who created us and knows everything?

Unbridled Praise

Give thanks to the God of heaven, for
his steadfast love endures forever.

Psalms 136:26 ESV

Come into the Kingdom of God and prepare to be overwhelmed; overwhelmed by God's enduring mercy, His faithful love, His steadfast love, and His everlasting lovingkindness. When you experience the unfailing love, mercy and kindness of God, the only response is praise. There are times when praise should be unbridled. "Then David danced before the Lord with all his might" (2 Samuel 6:14). Scripture says David leaped and whirled before the Lord, promising to be "even more undignified than this" as he praised the One who anointed him and gave him reasons to praise daily.

Psalm 136 is a Hallel, a song of praise, one of many recorded by David and other psalmists. It recounts the many ways that God is worthy of praise, as Creator, Deliverer, Shepherd, the One who continually cares for His people and gives them a heritage in Him. It is a reminder that we need to remember the many ways God is worthy of praise in our lives, and offer that praise by the words of our lips, by the way we live our lives and by how we use the many gifts He has given us.

We praise Him as Creator. Without Him there is no life. Look around at the majesty of His earthly creations and praise. Touch the toes of a newborn and praise. Hold the hand of an elderly person and praise God for the life lived, the knowledge learned and the blessings bestowed. Stand quietly on a clear night, look up and see the stars, the moon and constellations. Look in the mirror and see what He has done. Remember your new life in Him. Praise.

We praise Him as Deliverer. Look down through history and remember how He has been the faithful Father to His people. He brought the Israelites out of Egypt. He delivered the Jewish people into their own country. He prepared a way and delivered you into His kingdom. Throughout your life He has been constantly delivering you from oppression, delivering you into His bosom of protection. Praise.

We praise Him as the One who continually cares for His children, extending mercy and grace where none is warranted. He is always caring for us, giving us undeserved gifts: the child we prayed for, the job we wanted, the house we didn't know we needed. He grows us, disciplining us when needed, but walking with us in our pain, gently guiding us back onto the path of righteousness. He positions us in His kingdom, gives us gifts to use in His work, and places brothers and sisters around us to grow with us and love us on the way to eternity. Praise.

We praise Him for the heritage He has given. We are joint-heirs with Christ. We are new creatures. We carry the righteousness of Christ even though we have no right to it. He sees us as His children, He calls us His own. He promises us eternity with Him, in a place where sorrow will never again prevail. Though death may overtake us in this life, it has no claim on us and only opens a door to eternity. For His children, death is only a transition to the promised home with Him. Praise.

But as it is written: "Eye has not seen, nor ear heard, Nor have entered into the heart of man The things which God has prepared for those who love Him" (1 Corinthians 2:9). Praise.

* * *

Time in His Word:

Read Psalm 136; 1 Thessalonians 5:16–18,

Prayer:

Father open our eyes to see Your matchless gifts. Open our hearts to praise You, not just with our words, but with our lives, our movements, our songs. Let Your praise inhabit our being. May others see the joy and know You through our praise. Let there be no shame in our praise, just joyful, jubilant, unbridled praise, for You alone are worthy. In the name of Jesus Christ. Amen.

Meditations and Journaling:

Write your own song of praise to the Creator, the Deliverer, the One who cares for us and gives us a heritage.

Ebed-Melech

"I will deliver you from the hand of the wicked, And
I will redeem you from the grip of the terrible."

God's love is wrapped up in His faithfulness toward us. In fact, in each of His characteristics we see His love: in His justice, His mercy, His consistency, His tenderness. Sometimes that love sneaks up on you and catches you unaware. When it does, it is a sweet presence, a sweet sense leaving you with moments of preciousness, knowing once again just how much He cares for you personally. I'm thinking that the prophet Jeremiah and Ebed-Melech might have been caught off guard by the presence of God's love in His faithfulness toward them.

Jeremiah was a faithful prophet of the Lord. He suffered a great deal as a result of his faithfulness, finding his life in danger more than once. In Jeremiah 38 we find Jeremiah lingering in the mire of a dungeon with no food to sustain him, destined to die of starvation. He had been scorned by the king's advisors because of the prophecies he spoke concerning the future of the city. The advisors and princes convinced the king to put him away to silence him so the people and the men of war would not be discouraged by his prophecies. The king gave in to their demands, giving control over Jeremiah's future to them. Scripture says "They let Jeremiah down with ropes. And in the dungeon there was no water, but mire. So Jeremiah sank in the mire" (Jeremiah 38:6).

Ebed-Melech, an Ethiopian eunuch, petitioned the king for Jeremiah's release, telling the king that Jeremiah would surely die in that place. The king instructed Ebed-Melech to take others and rescue Jeremiah from the dungeon. Ebed-Melech took thirty men and pulled Jeremiah up from the mire. Scripture does not tell us of any special relationship between Jeremiah and Ebed-Melech, or of the reason that an Ethiopian eunuch would have such access or influence with the king, but Jeremiah is released and it appears that is the end of the story. God's faithfulness toward his prophet is evident in his deliverance.

We do not always credit the hand of God's love when we are delivered from a situation. Our immediate emotions are relief and gratitude. We don't stop to ponder the love that surrounds our release; mostly we are just happy to be free of the situation. But God's love is ever-present, underlying His purpose for allowing our situation and our release. Like Jesus, Jeremiah's desire was to do the will of the Father, to deliver the message God commissioned him to speak. His faithfulness frequently put him in peril, and Jeremiah may have rightfully wondered each time whether that situation would be the one that would end his life. But he carried a burden, like a burning fire, to speak the words of God, so he persevered in spite of the dangers (Jeremiah 20:9).

Ebed-Melech might also have considered his petition to the king and his rescue of Jeremiah to be only a part of his day's work and a rightful duty. But God remembers His servants and those who care for 'even the least of them.' He also looks into the motive and the heart behind the deed. In His justice, nothing goes unnoticed. Just one chapter over, in Jeremiah chapter 39, we see God's unanticipated response to Ebed-Melech's actions.

In fulfillment of the prophetic words spoken by Jeremiah, God pronounced destruction on Jerusalem because of their unfaithfulness. Jerusalem is besieged by Babylon, the king's house is burned, his sons killed and the walls of Jerusalem broken down. In the midst of the city's destruction God sent Jeremiah to say this to Ebed-Melech: "For I will surely deliver you, and you shall not fall by the sword; but your life shall be as a prize to you, because you have put your trust in Me," says the Lord' " (Jeremiah 39:18). Because of his trust in God and his reverence for the work assigned to Jeremiah by God, he was rewarded with his life for his small act of deliverance. Neither Jeremiah or Ebed-Melech were forgotten in their situations.

Today you may need to be delivered from a situation. Please know that your circumstances have not gone unnoticed by our faithful God. In His love, He will deliver you. Very likely there is an Ebed-Melech petitioning God on your behalf right now, someone you may not know or never would have guessed to be involved in your situation. Trust in God's love toward you, His sovereignty over your situation. Wait on your promised deliverance.

* * *

Time in His Word:

Read Jeremiah chapters 38 and 39 and record your thoughts

Prayer:

Father, we thank You for deliverance. You have delivered us from our life of sin, from the strongholds that held us back from worship. You saw our situation and stepped in with Your powerful right hand and pulled us out. Thank You Father! There is none like You; no one who is powerful enough to deliver completely. We have been deceived by many who promised freedom, but You, Oh Lord, are the One we place our trust in now and forevermore. Thank You for deliverance. In the name of Jesus Christ. Amen.

Meditation and Journaling:

What situation are you currently facing?
When did God last deliver you from a situation?
What have you done, now or in the past, to deserve deliverance?
Are you doubting His ability or willingness to rescue you today? Why?

DAY 17

Trials, Tests, Troubles and Temptations

I have not departed from his commands, but have
treasured his words more than daily food. But once
he has made his decision, who can change his mind?
Whatever he wants to do, he does. So he will do to me
whatever he has planned. He controls my destiny.

JOB 23:12–14 NLT

God's perfect love was present with Adam and Eve in the garden of Eden. However, His love did not prevent trouble and temptation. God's path to redemption runs parallel with Satan's desire to run us off the road of obedience, landing us smack dab in the middle of trouble. Sometimes trouble hits us out of nowhere and we have no way of knowing where it came from. We can choose to respond in humility and obedience to the God who loves us, or not.

Job, a man of God, found himself in such a situation. He was living life, enjoying his family, worshipping his God faithfully, and suddenly, trouble - trouble on a magnitude most will never know. Within moments, he lost his family, his home, his reputation, and his livelihood. Job had no way of knowing where the trouble came from, but his heartfelt response was to acknowledge the sovereignty of the God he worshipped and loved. He acknowledged God's right to be present in his life and make decisions. "Then Job arose and tore his robe and shaved his head and fell on the ground and worshiped. And he said, "Naked I came from my mother's womb, and naked shall I return. The Lord gave, and the Lord has taken away; blessed be the name of the Lord. In all this Job did not sin nor charge God with wrong" (Job 1:20–22 ESV).

OLIVIA DAVENPORT

Job did not blame God, rant at God, or attempt to bargain. He did not remind God that he served Him faithfully, was acknowledged by others for his faith, or that he 'deserved' better. He did not bring a sense of entitlement into the matter. We can know that he shed tears as he mourned and worshipped. In genuine humility, Job acknowledged God's right in his life. Later, when he was struck in his body with boils from the top of his head to the bottom of his feet, he wished for death, lamenting the day he was born. He heard others tell him his suffering was the result of sin and he questioned himself, but he did not blame God.

As Job looked back over his life for iniquities to answer the question of why he was suffering, he also questioned God, wanting to know the 'why' of his sufferings. In his questionings, there was never a moment when he lost faith or failed to acknowledge God's sovereign right to intervene in his life. The character of humility was always present. Humility is the understanding of sovereignty – looking at God with reverence, honor and respect -a 'big God, little me' understanding. He is the potter; we are the clay.

Troubles in our lives sometimes come as a consequence of our sins, God's desire to grow or test us, or God's desire to display His mercy through our circumstances. We may never know the reason for a specific trouble on this side of heaven, but we can trust the heart of our God to know that the trouble He allows in the life of His children will always result in their growth and will never come from God's failure to love us completely and know what is best for us. Our faith rests on this truth.

While he could have accepted the reasonings of his four friends who came to mourn with him, Job still looked to God for answers. God answered Job, but Job would never know that his troubles were the proof of God's word to Satan that His servant Job was upright, blameless and feared God. Instead, God answered Job with a chorus of sovereignty that left Job speechless and awed. He was able to 'see' the God who had the sovereign right to do whatever he chose to do (Job 42:5–6).

Trouble and temptations come to each one of us, not always of our choosing, but they always present us with an opportunity. With every trouble or temptation, we have an opportunity to honor God with our obedience, or to dishonor Him when we choose to follow our own path. As our experience and history with God grows, we are more able to trust

Him in the midst of suffering, even when we do not know the reason for the trial. Our suffering calls us to a deeper level of trust in Him. Hold fast to the truth of God's goodness and integrity toward you.

* * *

Time in His Word:

Read Job chapter 1 and chapter 42

Prayer:

Lord, help us in our suffering to trust Your goodness toward us. Please hear our hearts when we pray and walk with us through the trials. Help us to grow in Your truth, not giving into the lie that we can make our own truth. In the name of Jesus Christ. Amen.

Meditations and Journaling:

How is your faith today? Place yourself in Job's shoes. How do you believe you would respond if God stretched out His hand and allowed all that you have to be taken away? Will you curse God and lose faith over material and physical things?

The Absolute Privilege

> *And Hannah answered and said, "No, my*
> *lord, I am a woman of sorrowful spirit. I have*
> *drunk neither wine nor intoxicating drink, but*
> *have poured out my soul before the Lord.*
>
> 1 SAMUEL 1:15

When was the last time you 'poured out your soul' before the Lord?

Perhaps it was at a moment of complete sorrow, unfathomable brokenness or absolute surrender: "God, I can't do it anymore." That's where Hannah found herself. She was the incredibly loved wife of Elkanah, a man who loved the Lord and faithfully served Him.

Hannah was barren. In her time and culture, barrenness was considered a curse. Despite the faithful love of her husband, Hannah was empty, desolate and destitute of mind. She sought God's hand of provision in prayer. Her prayer was not a simple "Oh, by the way, Lord" prayer. No, she was in the trenches, on her knees, calling out with gut-wrenching sobs to the Lord of heaven, the only One who could reverse her situation. Ever been there?

Prayer. Sometimes we take it for granted. We pray regularly – sometimes out of habit, sometimes in a moment of desperate need, sometimes just as we work through our day. But, how often do you grasp the magnitude of being able to reach out in prayer to our omnipotent, omnipresent, omniscient God? How often do you take the opportunity to deepen your relationship with God through prayer? The One who loves you most has granted to you the privilege of being able to reach His ears and His heart anytime, anywhere. That's what Hannah did. She accepted that gift of love and ran with it. She prayed with all her heart and God answered. Prayer is not only a game changer in our situations, it is a relationship changer when we surrender ourselves to God in a two-way conversation that allows us to hear His heart.

As you reach to the only One who can completely understand your requests and search your heart, grasp the love that is inherent in the gift of prayer. God loved us beyond creation and beyond our sin, allowing us into His presence to talk with Him about anything. He never posts an out of order sign, or a going on vacation notice. He never stops hearing our petitions and healing our hearts. After her time of prayer, scripture notes that "So the woman went her way and ate, and her face was no longer sad "(1 Samuel 1:18). On the surface, her situation had not changed, but her time in prayer had given her peace based on her confidence in the heart of God.

God answers prayers - in His time and in His way. In time, Hannah conceived and bore the prophet Samuel. Scripture also tells us that she later bore three sons and two daughters (1 Samuel 2:21). Every prayer uttered by a believer is answered. That is more than we can fathom, more than we deserve. Yet, in God's graciousness, He bends to hear His children and He answers our prayers. Sometimes His answer is 'yes,' sometimes it is 'no,' sometimes it is 'not now.' He answers each prayer for our good. He knows what we need, and He provides abundantly in His time, in His way. Sometimes we refuse to accept His answer, getting in the way, insisting that God respond to our prayers only in the way we define, not accepting that His ways are best.

The privilege of prayer is sometimes taken for granted, but our right to sit in the presence of God and pour out our hearts to Him is embedded in the privileges that come with acceptance of His Son Jesus Christ as Savior. No one can take that absolute privilege from you, but you can lose out on the benefits of prayer when you choose to handle situations on your own, leaning to your own understanding and failing to benefit from His wisdom and guidance. Hannah yielded herself in prayer and was privileged to see God work in her situation. God offers to work in your situations today. Pray without ceasing.

* * *

Time in His Word:

Read 1 Samuel chapter 1 and 2:1–10; 1 Thessalonians 5:16–19

Prayer:

Oh, heavenly Father, we thank You for the gift of prayer and the privilege to come into Your presence with our every concern. You are the God of blessings, but we want to bless you with our praise and gratitude and obedience. Help us to grow in our fellowship with You through the gift of prayer. Let our time with You become water to our thirsty soul, nourishing us each day and fueling us for the battles of this life. In the name of Jesus Christ. Amen.

Meditations and Journaling:

Do you view prayer as a privilege, a necessity, or a duty? Would your answer be supported by the amount of time you spend in prayer and the depth of your relationship with the Father?

Unwavering Faithful Love

Moreover I will make a covenant of peace with them,
and it shall be an everlasting covenant with them;
I will establish them and multiply them, and I will
set My sanctuary in their midst forevermore.

EZEKIEL 37:26

The Old Testament gives us a vivid picture of God's dealings with the nation of Israel. He calls them His own, loves them, teaches them, protects them, chastises them, punishes them, and restores them. He punishes those who mistreat Israel. Although their cycle of disobedience is repeated over and over, He never turns from them, but continues to love them because they are His children. This is His character and relationship with all of His children, all those who are children of faith, with hearts sold out to Him. He is ever the loving father, seeking to reconcile all of His children to Him; seeking their obedience, righteousness, and holiness. God's love for His children is active, not passive.

Over and over the nation of Israel chose their own path. They worshipped other gods, arousing the anger of Jehovah God. He allowed their foolishness for a time, sending prophet after prophet to speak His truth to them. He called out their adultery with other gods and pronounced a penalty: "Therefore thus says the Lord God: Because you have forgotten me and cast me behind your back, you yourself must bear the consequences of your lewdness and whoring" (Ezekiel 23:35 ESV). Sometimes the nation would turn back to Him in halfhearted worship, but they did not remove the high places that were symbols of their unfaithfulness to Him. As He does with us, God never stopped sending truth to them. He never stopped loving them. He never stopped seeking their hearts.

There was a time of reckoning for their disobedience. God punished His children. He allowed the surrounding nations to defeat them in battle, take them captive and oppress them. Because of their disobedience and hardheadedness, the nation of Israel was captured by the Assyrians, the nation of Judah captured by the Babylonians. Even as they were in captivity, God sent prophets. The prophets Ezekiel and Daniel were taken away as captives along with the multitudes, speaking God's truth to them, even as they were held by a hostile nation. Because of God's faithful character, there was <u>never</u> a time when the nation was unable to hear God's voice and know that they were His beloved.

In time there was restoration. The captives returned home to their land and began the process of rebuilding. Once again, God sent men who would share truth. Nehemiah records a great revival, a time when the returning captives heard the truth and responded to God's word: "Then Nehemiah the governor, Ezra the priest and scribe, and the Levites who were interpreting for the people said to them, "Don't mourn or weep on such a day as this! For today is a sacred day before the Lord your God." For the people had all been weeping as they listened to the words of the Law" (Nehemiah 8:9 NLT).

Even as the events of history unfolded with the nation of Israel, God was actively making the way for the Messiah to come. He did not forget His purpose, His plan or His promise. He did not get sidetracked by the disobedience of men. This Messiah would provide the path to everlasting redemption. Through forty-two generations, from Abraham to David and from David to Jesus the Messiah, the plan unfolded, in spite of man's unfaithfulness to God (Matthew 1:17). He is faithful when we are not.

In our lives today His love never wavers. We are His children. We fall, He punishes and restores. We are contrite over our sin, but in time we fall again. We repent and He restores again. Love we do not deserve. Mercy we can't imagine. Grace for each new day.

* * *

Time in His Word:

Read Romans 8:35–39

Prayer:

Heavenly Father, because we are unfaithful, we cannot fathom Your faithfulness. Forgive us. Teach us to understand Your faithfulness. Teach us Your quality of faithfulness. Open our eyes to see Your faithfulness and consistency in our lives. Help us to praise and glorify You for Your faithfulness and allow us to tell others about our God who will never leave us. Let our lives reflect the confidence that comes from knowing our faithful Father. In the name of Jesus Christ. Amen.

Meditations and Journaling:

Our concepts of faithfulness and unfaithfulness often come from the world. Contrast the world's concept of faithfulness to what our God offers, considering how you have been impacted by both. Remember a specific instance of His faithfulness in your life.

DAY 20
Everlasting Presence

Do not be afraid or discouraged, for the Lord will
personally go ahead of you. He will be with you;
he will neither fail you nor abandon you."

DEUTERONOMY 31:8 NLT

Our Father God is <u>never</u> going to leave you or stop loving you. Imagine the security of that statement. The word 'never' is absolute and cannot be applied to many things. But because God is absolute, we can boldly say He will <u>never</u> default on His promises because His character is tied to His promises. He is the only One who sees all, knows all, and is always present. We can trust the promise of His everlasting presence.

We spend a lifetime looking for someone who will be consistently stable for us, always present, always in our corner. Unfortunately, with man/woman, providing that everlasting presence and stability for someone else is rarely possible, regardless of the desire to do so. People die, circumstances change, and suddenly the permanence and stability you counted on is gone. But God will <u>never</u> leave you, forsake you, or stop loving you.

Throughout scripture, in many ways, He repeated the promise of His everlasting presence and protection. He did not forsake Adam and Eve when they ate the forbidden fruit. He clothed them, protected them from the tree of life, and escorted them from the garden, but not from His presence. He repeated the same promise to Jacob, to Joshua, to Solomon and He says the same to you. (See Genesis 28:15, Joshua 1:5, 1 Chronicles 28:20)

He actively demonstrated His presence and protection to the Israelites as they left Egypt with Pharaoh's men in hot pursuit. He opened the waters for the Israelites to pass through and closed the waters upon the pursuing

Egyptian warriors. As they traveled through the desert to the promised land, God provided a cloud by day and fire by night – not just protection from the heat of the day and the chill of the night, but guidance for their travels (Exodus 13:21–22). When the cloud lifted, they moved. When the cloud did not lift, they remained in their camping place. (Numbers 9:17–19) God provided manna for their meals and sustained them with great mercies throughout a time when they challenged His love with consistent disobedience. Scripture says "For forty years you sustained them in the wilderness, and they lacked nothing. Their clothes did not wear out, and their feet did not swell!" (Nehemiah 9:21 NLT). His presence. His protection. His guidance. Promises fulfilled.

God has not changed (Malachi 3:6). His promise of everlasting presence, protection and guidance are for you today. "So we may boldly say: "The Lord is my helper; I will not fear. What can man do to me?" (Hebrews 13:6). As His child, committed to His Son Jesus Christ, you can relax in knowing that nothing in this world comes to you except that which He has allowed for your growth and your good. The plans of the enemy are always filtered through His hands for His children. The circumstances of your life are never out of His hands. Rest in this assurance. His presence is actively with you each day in the presence of His Holy Spirit, living within you, going before you in your circumstances, leading you, guiding you into knowledge of who He is and an understanding of His ways. Circumstances may cause you to be afraid, but your confidence in the reality of His presence and love will enable you to face those circumstances knowing He will bring you out. Whatever circumstances you face, you face in His presence. The battle is not yours; you do not have to fight; the battle is already won.

* * *

Time in His Word:

Read Psalm 37:25, 94:14; 2 Corinthians 4:8–10

Prayer:

Oh Lord Jehovah, Our Father in heaven, we come before You in our circumstances, with our fear, acknowledging our lack of faith. Please help our unbelief Father. Show Yourself powerful in our circumstances. Once again, Father, let us know You are here, that You are over all and in all. Help us to remember Your presence, Your power, Your protection. Lead and guide us into Your will, Father and let the darkness of our fear in these circumstances leave us. In the way that only You can, Father bring us Your peace. Help us to trust Father. In the name of our precious Lord and Savior, Jesus Christ. Amen.

Meditations and Journaling:

Have you had times when you felt abandoned? Have you had times when you felt abandoned by God? Think of the times when you were assured of His presence. How has He proven himself faithful to you?

But God demonstrates His own love toward us, in that while we were still sinners, Christ died for us.

ROMANS 5:8

Chapter 3
EVIDENCE OF LOVE

Learning outcomes for chapter 3 (Days 21-30)

- ✓ Understand the many ways God makes our journey easier through His offerings of hope, forgiveness, reconciliation and gifts given at salvation.

- ✓ Know that God will always confront sin because He loves the sinner

- ✓ Understand the way He draws each of us into an individual relationship with Him

- ✓ Stand in awe of the many ways a believer can experience intimacy with our Father God

- ✓ Understand that each day is changed when you live with an eternal perspective

The Gift of Hope

*The people who walk in darkness will see
a great light. For those who live in a land
of deep darkness, a light will shine.*

ISAIAH 9:2 NLT

We live in a world that is too easily beset by hopelessness. Because of technological advances, we can see immediately, up close and personal, all the tragedies that happen not just to our next-door neighbors, but to the families in nations half-way around the globe. We not only get to hear the news; we get to see the raw unfiltered emotions that go with the circumstances. We see the devastation of war, the carnage of natural disasters and the grief that goes with loss of life. We try to understand the unthinkable: senseless murders of innocent children, a world gone crazy with lust and the unbalanced disposition of goods that leaves some with egregious wealth and others homeless. And there is more, always more… It leaves us shaking our heads, wondering where we are going as a nation, as a society, as a world. We wonder about the moral inclination of many and see the depravity in the logic applied to everyday life. Sometimes we succumb to hopelessness, wondering if things can get worse, and then they do get worse. Or so it seems.

God never intended for us to feel hopeless. He has always offered hope. He promised a seed of mankind that would bruise the head of the serpent, in time bringing an end to this trouble-filled world. Prophecies foretold the end of grief, the coming of a Messiah who would change the world, who would bring light to a dark world. The Messiah would come from heaven, with power to cause God's will to be done on earth as it is in heaven. The Messiah would bring an end to wars and rumors of wars. The promised Messiah will bring hope and "He will bring justice to the poor of the people; He will save the children of the needy, And will break in pieces the oppressor" (Psalms 72:4).

The pages of scripture promise hope. God never forgets His promises; He is a covenant- keeping God. As the time drew near, the angel Gabriel visited a young virgin named Mary, telling her she was highly favored and would conceive in her womb and deliver the promised hope of all mankind, fulfilling the promises made to Abraham, Isaac, and Jacob and continuing the kingly throne of David. "And behold, you will conceive in your womb and bring forth a Son, and shall call His name Jesus. He will be great, and will be called the Son of the Highest; and the Lord God will give Him the throne of His father David. And He will reign over the house of Jacob forever, and of His kingdom there will be no end" (Luke 1:31–33).

Immanuel, the Hebrew name meaning "God with us," perfectly reflects God's plan of hope. Jesus, Immanuel, came to earth to dwell with His people, to offer the only perfect sacrifice that would appease a Holy God. Born to die for us. Born to bring hope. Born to redeem us from a cycle of sin that ends in death. Born to offer us His perfect righteousness in exchange for our sin. Perfect hope offered freely by our loving God.

Jesus is the light that dispels darkness and gloom. Hopelessness finds us crouching in corners contemplating ways to end this life. The hope of Jesus brings light into the darkness of our worlds and offers a way to keep going forward. At the right time, God sent His Son to bring us everlasting hope. At the right time, God's promises and prophecies were fulfilled in the coming of Jesus. At the right time, God will end the cycle of sin and bring His children into eternity where hopelessness cannot enter.

* * *

Time in His Word:

Read Psalm 72; Isaiah 9:1–7; Hebrews 6:13–20

Prayer:

Father, thank You for loving us so much that You never left us. Thank You for sending hope into our lives. Thank You for the person who shared

Jesus with us. Your hope changed our lives. Give us the courage to end someone else's hopelessness by sharing the message of Jesus. In the name of Jesus Christ. Amen.

Meditations and Journaling:

Ask God to reveal to you someone who needs to hear the message of hope. Prepare in prayer and share Jesus with someone who is hopeless today. Tell them how your hopelessness was turned into hope.

The Savior Comes

But when the fullness of the time had come, God sent forth His Son, born of a woman, born under the law, to redeem those who were under the law, that we might receive the adoption as sons.

GALATIANS 4:4–5

If I could draw a line from the beginning of Genesis to the New Testament accounts of Jesus' birth, that line would chronicle the faithfulness of God's promises to redeem mankind. Through the patriarchs of old, the kingly line of David, and the prophets who foretold Jesus' coming, we see a steady march through history to God's promised redemption. The line would not stop at the birth, death and resurrection of Christ, but would continue, through the rapture, the tribulation, the Messianic reign, the final judgment and into eternity. God's timing is not ours, His ways are not our ways, but His timing is best.

In the fullness of time, Mary gave birth to God's Son, conceived of the Holy Spirit, and placed Him in a manger. Here was hope wrapped in a tiny baby. She gave birth to the promised Messiah and Satan upped his game, even though his best game would never stop God's plan for you and me. From Bethlehem to Egypt to Nazareth in Judea, our path to salvation was revealed. Before time, God had this plan in place to redeem you and me from hopelessness, from certain death promised with the first bite of fruit. "Because God's children are human beings—made of flesh and blood—the Son also became flesh and blood. For only as a human being could he die, and only by dying could he break the power of the devil, who had the power of death" (Hebrews 2:14 NLT).

This is hope, not the futile longings we express so often, hoping for this or that material thing, but HOPE that is certain. This is HOPE that is grounded in the love, righteousness, faithfulness and holiness of God's character. This is HOPE that only the God who can speak galaxies into existence offers. HOPE arrived in the person of Jesus Christ; certain salvation for all who receive Him as Savior. This is God's active love on display for all to see. This HOPE was robed in the person of Jesus as an infant, as a child of twelve sitting in His Father's house questioning the scribes, changing water into wine, helping the blind to see, and the lame to walk. Jesus Christ, God incarnate, HOPE personified, love magnified.

Jesus came with the purpose, power and passion to complete the work His Father gave Him to do (John 17:4). He called and trained twelve to establish His church on earth. His church offers the sure promise of heaven and eternity with God, but also offers innumerable gifts to the believer on earth. We are saved, forgiven, redeemed, reconciled to God, and adopted as sons. We are made new in Him. Our time on earth is not wasted.

On earth, in His church, Christ offers gifts that prepare us for eternity. In His church we see the full heart of God on display. Earth is the training ground for our lives with other believers in heaven. Earth offers us a preview of what heaven has in store. "Now we see things imperfectly as in a cloudy mirror, but then we will see everything with perfect clarity. All that I know now is partial and incomplete, but then I will know everything completely, just as God now knows me completely" (1 Corinthians 13:12 NLT).

* * *

Time in His Word:

Read Hebrews 2:14–17

Prayer:

Our Father, thank You for not discarding us in our sin and for loving us enough to send a Savior. We praise You for Your faithfulness to Your promises and to us. In the name of Jesus Christ. Amen.

Meditations and Journaling:

God sent a Savior for you. He prepared a place in His kingdom for you. Meditate on the magnitude of His love for just you. Will you let that love in? Will you let it change you?

The Balm in Gilead

But he was wounded for our transgressions; he was crushed for our iniquities; upon him was the chastisement that brought us peace, and with his stripes we are healed.

ISAIAH 53:5 ESV

Only because of the wounds of Jesus Christ, are we offered reconciliation to God and the healing of forgiveness. "For God's will was for us to be made holy by the sacrifice of the body of Jesus Christ, once for all time" (Hebrews 10:10 NLT). His sacrificial death opened the door for us to be presented as righteous before a loving God. We wear the righteousness of Jesus as we are reconciled to God and cleansed of our sinful state. The law defined sin for us but we are powerless on our own to erase that sin – our sincere desire, earnest willpower and valiant effort are not enough to cleanse us from sin. Jesus, once and for all, presented Himself on our behalf to erase the sin debt we could do nothing about. His atoning sacrifice was accepted on our behalf by our heavenly Father.

In the Bible, Gilead is the place where the tree sap called the balm of Gilead is produced. This balm, like an ointment, had healing powers. Gilead is also the place where many people fled for safety – the Israelites from Philistine solders, King David from Absalom (2 Samuel 17–19). Jacob fled from Laban to the mountains of Gilead, and reconciled with his brother Esau in Mahanaim of Gilead (Genesis 31:21, 32:1). Like those fleeing to Gilead, we flee from our state of unrighteousness into the arms of our loving God. He offers us sanctuary and power over our sins.

Our reconciliation to God and forgiveness of our sins, purchased by Christ, is our balm in Gilead. It is our way to peace with God and with ourselves. Like a healing balm, forgiveness soothes, takes away the pain of our actions and the actions of others. Our forgiveness frees us to live in right relationship with God and with others. Whether we ask out loud or not, we all will need and want a second chance, a third chance, or a hundredth chance. Because of His sacrifice, we never have to wonder if that forgiveness is ours.

As the prophet Jeremiah mourned for the backsliding of the people about to be captured by the Babylonians, he asked: "Is there no medicine in Gilead? Is there no physician there? Why is there no healing for the wounds of my people?" (Jeremiah 8:22 NLT). Because of their sin and unrepentant hearts, there was no balm to change the upcoming captivity promised by God to the people of Judah, but we indeed have a balm in Gilead. Jesus, our balm, has opened the door to peace with God. He stands at the door, waiting for us to partake of all that His sacrifice offered. He is the physician eager to heal our wounds and walk with us into new life in His kingdom.

"For it pleased the Father that in Him all the fullness should dwell, and by Him to reconcile all things to Himself, by Him, whether things on earth or things in heaven, having made peace through the blood of His cross" (Colossians 1:19–20). Jesus is the only lasting balm needed to heal the wounds inflicted by this life. The world offers temporary fixes for our hurts, but only His healing suffices for eternity. We are the beneficiaries of the wounds of Jesus Christ. Our healing is ongoing. Each day we are privileged to draw closer in relationship to God. We are privileged to share the source of our healing with others. We are privileged to rejoice in the healing balm of His presence with us. Yes, indeed, for the one who will choose to have fellowship with Jesus, there is a balm in Gilead, healing for the people of God.

* * *

Time in His Word:

Read Colossians 1:19–23; 1 Peter 2:24–25;

Prayer:

We thank you Father that You are patient with us; that You have brought us home to be always in Your presence. In the name of Jesus Christ who healed us with His blood. Amen.

Meditations and Journaling:

Meditate on all the ways you have experienced His healing as you grow in relationship with Jesus. How has your healing impacted others in your circle of family and friends?

A Chance Encounter?

But He needed to go through Samaria.

JOHN 4:4

On the way from Judea to Galilee, Jesus needed to go through Samaria. Traditionally, because of cultural distinctions, Jews did not associate with Samaritans. Jesus, however, did not hold to cultural distinctions and traditions. He came to do the work of His Father and would not allow those humanly inspired and contrived limitations to get in the way of the work He came to do. So, on the way from Judea to Galilee, Jesus went through Samaria, following the shortest route. Fully human, He became weary and took a rest by Jacob's Well in the City of Sychar. Fully divine, He knew of the divine appointment with the next woman to visit the well to draw water.

His request to the Samaritan woman for water became a discipleship moment. She challenged His request because He was a Jewish man asking a Samaritan woman for water because there was normally no association between the two, either on the cultural/ethnic level or the male/female level. Overlooking her questioning, Jesus offered her more than she had ever experienced: "If you knew the gift of God, and who it is who says to you, 'Give Me a drink,' you would have asked Him, and He would have given you living water" (John 4:10). Only able to see the physical in front of her, she reminded Jesus that He had nothing to draw water with. Jesus persisted, drawing on the spiritual needs we all have, offering her living water, water that would always satisfy, reaching out to nourish others. Jesus reached into the deepest places of her heart, not judging her life, but revealing her needs. I believe His truth allowed Her transparency.

Something happened when she experienced the love and welcome that He offered without judging her past. Beyond revealing Himself as Messiah and accepting her proclamation of Him as a prophet, He crossed all the cultural boundaries to draw her into His kingdom.

For this Samaritan woman, a lifetime of striving for truth and love came to an abrupt end in a 'chance' encounter with Jesus near Jacob's Well. He <u>needed</u> to go through Samaria – for her, for the town where He spent the next two days revealing the truth of His Father's kingdom, offering living water to all who would accept. Many believed because of her word about the prophet, but many more believed because of His own words to them (John 4:39–41).

By all accounts this looked like a 'chance' encounter, but like every encounter in Jesus' years of ministry, it was purposeful and intentional. Jesus offered salvation and new life in every encounter, seeking the one who would believe. "The people who walked in darkness Have seen a great light; Those who dwelt in the land of the shadow of death, Upon them a light has shined" (Isaiah 9:2). We dwell in the shadow of death, but He offers light to dispel those shadows.

He will not leave anyone out. He is chasing you today, offering you salvation, new life and a closer walk with Him. Encounters that you think are chance, are not. Circumstances in your life are not accidents. They are God moments intended for you, designed to draw you into closer fellowship with the God who loves you intensely. Sometimes those encounters are not comfortable, touchy-feely moments, but only the One who created you knows what will draw you closer. Let your striving come to an end today. Relax into His presence.

* * *

Time in His Word:

Read John 4:1–42

Prayer:

Father in Heaven, Thank You for drawing me into Your presence and ending my striving. Please continue to draw me closer by Your truth. May my heart always resonate with your presence. Allow me to see Your light, to drink of Your living water, and to worship You in Spirit and in truth. In the name of Jesus Christ. Amen.

Meditations and Journaling:

Like the Samaritan woman, do you sometimes get sidetracked by the physical? Think of the ways you substitute physical things for deeper, more meaningful moments with God. How can you change that to move closer in relationship with Him?

His Providential Care

*I will be your God throughout your lifetime— until your
hair is white with age. I made you, and I will care
for you. I will carry you along and save you.*

ISAIAH 46:4 NLT

God's providential care covers all of mankind. He extends His love to
everyone. "For He makes His sun rise on the evil and on the good, and
sends rain on the just and on the unjust" (Matthew 5:45). God offers the
promise of eternity to all, but some will reject that promise and choose
to live without all that He offers. They will continue to rely on chance,
content to expect good luck and coincidence to guide them to a prosperous
future while at the same time experiencing the goodness of His providential
care for all.

For those who accept God's invitation, extended through the death
and resurrection of Jesus Christ, there is the benefit of His sovereign
providential care in their lives. God is active in the life of the believer,
working to fulfill His purposes through the one who is willing to be used
in His kingdom. "And we know that God causes everything to work
together for the good of those who love God and are called according to his
purpose for them" (Romans 8:28 NLT). There is no luck, no randomness,
no coincidence in the life of a believer. Everything in the life of the believer
in Jesus Christ is filtered through the hands of a loving God so that even
the worst circumstances result in increased faith and unforeseen gifts
measured in the economy of eternity.

Rahab's life is an example of the sovereign providential care of God.
When the Israelites prepared to cross over into the promised land to

capture the land promised to them by God, Joshua sent two men ahead to spy out the City of Jericho. The spies went to Jericho and sought lodging at the home of Rahab the harlot. God meets all of us where we are, acknowledging our sin but offering a way out. As she hid them from the governing authorities in Jericho, Rahab's statement to the spies indicated that everyone in the City of Jericho knew the power of their God and was 'fainthearted' at the power of the God of the Israelites. The whole city was scared of what was to come; they knew destruction was near. "For we have heard how the Lord dried up the water of the Red Sea for you when you came out of Egypt, and what you did to the two kings of the Amorites who were on the other side of the Jordan, Sihon and Og, whom you utterly destroyed" (Joshua 2:10).

Her statement also indicated her faith in their God, and it was this faith that placed her in the providential care of God: "for the Lord your God, He is God in heaven above and on earth beneath" (Joshua 2:11). She trusted God to bring her out of the coming destruction and she asked for deliverance. Because of her faith, Rahab and all of her father's household were saved from the destruction of Jericho by the invading Israelites. When God meets us where we are, He places us into His care and moment by moment He grows our faith so that our heart's desire matches the desire of His heart. His goodness to us is overwhelming; we have never known a love like His. In time it becomes a small thing to give up the sin we've become so accustomed to in order to please Him.

Nothing else is told of Rahab outside the book of Joshua until we get to the Gospel of Matthew and find Rahab recorded in the genealogy of Jesus Christ: "Salmon begot Boaz by Rahab, ..." (Matthew 1:5). Her faith and trust allowed God to use her to fulfill His promise to all of us. Rahab, no longer named a harlot, had a part in the lineage of the Savior destined to crush the head of the serpent.

Are you trusting in luck today? Are you hoping that things will turn around for you simply by coincidence? Waiting for your ship to come in? Thinking all roads lead to heaven? There was no coincidence in the life of Rahab. It was her faith, not a coincidence, that her house was the house where travelers lodged and that she would receive the blessings of escape when the city was destroyed. You too can experience the blessings of escape from the haphazardness of luck when you place your life in the hands of

God's providential care. Allow Him to fill your life with His purpose. Place your faith in Jesus and find yourself in the center of God's sovereign providential care.

* * *

Time in His Word

Read Joshua chapters 1–3

Prayer

Father, I am thankful to be released from the tyranny of trying to run my own life, from the insecurity of my five-year plans. I am thankful that I can know Your goodness toward me. I understand that You allow me free will but that You already know the outcome and You have prepared a way out of my handmade messes. Thank You for being my loving parent, always there to guide me, lead me and walk beside me. Thank You that ALL things work for my good because I love You and place my life in Your hands. In the name of Jesus Christ. Amen.

Meditations and Journaling

What is the biggest mess you've made in your life? What has come out of that mess? Are you able to see God's hand in the outcome? How might others see you trusting God as you experience problems?

DAY 26
The Heart of God

And I heard a loud voice from heaven saying,
"Behold, the tabernacle of God is with men, and He
will dwell with them, and they shall be His people.
God Himself will be with them and be their God.

REVELATION 21:3

God has always chosen to dwell among His people. His desire is intimate relationship with you. He created Eve to meet Adam's desire for relationship. Made in His image, we desire intimate relationship also. In the garden, He walked with Adam and Eve in the cool of the day (Genesis 3:8). As the Israelite nation walked in the desert, He showed Himself in a cloud by day, and fire by night. His Spirit inhabited the Holy of Holies in the tabernacle, always with them. He loves you and desires to be present with you always. Zechariah 8 prophetically speaks of a time when God will dwell with His people in the midst of Jerusalem. Throughout scripture we see the desire of God's heart to dwell with His people. Over and over, He says in scripture "I will be their God and they will be my people."[1]

Jesus, God with us, walked on the earth, promising to send the Holy Spirit to dwell in believers after His ascension. Speaking to His disciples He tells them "Nevertheless, I tell you the truth: it is to your advantage that I go away, for if I do not go away, the Helper will not come to you. But if I go, I will send him to you" (John 16:7 ESV). He said that the coming Helper would not only dwell with them, but would be in them (John 14:17). Like the tabernacle's Holy of Holies, our bodies are the dwelling place, the temple of God's Holy Spirit. God's Spirit comes to inhabit believers at the moment they place their faith in Jesus Christ, a beautiful expression of God's love for each believer. In this we have been given a priceless gift – to know the mind of God and to be sharers of His Spirit.

Prior to Jesus sending the promised Holy Spirit, the Old Testament records many instances of the Holy Spirit 'coming upon' someone for the performance of a specific act or prophecy (Exodus 31:3–6). God's Spirit was active always, but not until Jesus sent the Holy Spirit was there an indwelling of God's Spirit in believers. Acts 1 records Jesus' direction to His disciples before His ascension, to wait at Jerusalem until the baptism of the Holy Spirit. The Holy Spirit came upon each of the disciples and they spoke in the native tongues of people from many nations visiting Jerusalem for Pentecost. Because of the manifestation of the Holy Spirit many people became believers on that day. The Holy Spirit is always active in convicting the hearts of unbelievers to know Jesus.

Of all the gifts we receive at salvation, His eternal presence in us is the gift that transforms us and grows us into who we are called to be in Him. Jesus said the Holy Spirit of God would testify of Him, comfort us, teach us, walk with us, and convict us of sin (John 14–15). Proverbs 3:6 says He will direct our paths. His Spirit in us will lead us in His ways and correct us when we falter. He is present with believers for each moment of each day, not just for the performance of a specific time of witnessing or other work that we perceive is related to Him. When we have wrong thoughts or are tempted to say or do things which do not bless Him, He is with us and we hear His voice. His presence is not temporary or transitory. He does not come and go – He is always with you. And, He will never leave you. That still small voice will lead you and guide you into all truth and will always testify of Jesus. "So I want you to know that no one speaking by the Spirit of God will curse Jesus, and no one can say Jesus is Lord, except by the Holy Spirit" (1 Corinthians 12:3 NLT).

God loves you and He desires to dwell in you for every step of this life. To know God is to know that His heart's desire is to have intimate fellowship with His people. On His final night, Jesus prayed for every believer, showing us once again the heart of God for every believer to be in intimate relationship and fellowship with God. "I am praying not only for these disciples but also for all who will ever believe in me through their message. I pray that they will all be one, just as you and I are one—as you are in me, Father, and I am in you. And may they be in us so that the world will believe you sent me" (John 17:20–21 NLT).

* * *

Time in His Word:

Read Ezekiel 37:26–28; Zechariah 8; John 14:18

Prayer:

Father, I thank You that I am never out of Your presence, that You know me fully and completely and yet You still love me. Thank You for Your Holy Spirit that directs and guides me as I navigate this life. Let me be attentive to your word through the Holy Spirit and help me to be obedient. Lead me so that I bring You glory always. In the name of Jesus Christ. Amen.

Meditations and Journaling:

When did you most recently hear the still small voice of God? Is your heart tuned to hear His voice, even in the most routine moments? Think about why it might be hard to believe how much you are loved by God. Pray to know how much He loves you, to be able to live in that reality and hear His voice.

DAY 27

A Higher Standard

And have you forgotten the exhortation that addresses you as sons? "My son, do not regard lightly the discipline of the Lord, nor be weary when reproved by him. For the Lord disciplines the one he loves, and chastises every son whom he receives."

Hebrews 12:5–6 ESV

Some believers think that the Christian walk is impossibly hard, that we are doomed to fail. Because of this thinking, they give up trying. It is true that God's ways are not our ways, and that His thoughts are not our thoughts (Isaiah 55:9), but He has given us the indwelling of His Holy Spirit to navigate the paths laid out before us. He does not expect us to know the secret things of God, but He has provided everything we need to know so we can walk faithfully before Him. "The Lord our God has secrets known to no one. We are not accountable for them, but we and our children are accountable forever for all that he has revealed to us, so that we may obey all the terms of these instructions" (Deuteronomy 29:29 NLT).

We have the mind of Christ (1Corinthians 2:16), and we have the Word of God revealed in the Holy Bible. We have been given clear instructions in His word for the things that remain in our spheres of influence and the things we are accountable for. God never leaves us in the dark, wondering which way to turn. Scripture is clear on His expectations.

Before the Israelites crossed over into the Promised Land, Moses reiterated the law for them. He laid out God's expectations clearly. He defined for them the blessings that would occur if they were obedient and the curses that would fall on them if they chose to be disobedient (Deuteronomy 28). All through the prophetic books of the Bible, God's prophets forewarned the nations of Judah and Israel about what would happen to their nations if they continued to disobey God. They laid out God's planned blessings if the nations would lay aside their idols and choose Him. The prophets also clearly stated God's love for them and that He would take back His children and punish their aggressors. God does not change; we also have been given clear instructions for walking this Christian walk and for knowing God's expectations and the consequences of disobedience.

But, like Paul stated in the book of Romans, there is another law at work in our members (Romans 7: 21–23). Responding to our natural inclinations, we succumb to temptation and willfully decide to do it our way. He holds us to a higher standard than the world around us - His standards of righteousness and holiness. Our independent actions lead God to discipline us and we also suffer the consequences of our sin. We are disciplined by the hand of a Father who loves us. Discipline without love is abuse. We are never abused by God. There is confrontation but no condemnation in His discipline. His loving discipline assures us that we belong to Him. "If God doesn't discipline you as he does all of his children, it means that you are illegitimate and are not really his children at all" (Hebrews 12:8 NLT).

Think of those who went before us – Moses, David, Peter, and others. Moses struck the rock in disobedience and was not allowed to go into the Promised Land. David sinned with Bathsheba and the child died. Peter denied Jesus and suffered agony of soul. But, in God's loving discipline we see the hand of God's mercy. Moses, David, Peter and others were not cast off from God's presence. They experienced God's displeasure and the resulting discipline but after a time they each experienced forgiveness and restoration. Moses led the Israelites to the Promised Land; David led a kingly monarch and Peter was restored by Jesus to feed His sheep. Their discipline and restoral refreshed them for the work God ordained them to do.

God looks at the overall intent of the heart and extends His love even in light of our constant failures. He chastens us for a time, but He always draws us gently back into fellowship with Him. God extends unconditional love even though we do not deserve it. We are His children. Our will fails, but His love and mercy never fail.

* * *

Time in His Word:

Read Hebrews 12:5–13

Prayer:

"Now may the God of peace— who brought up from the dead our Lord Jesus, the great Shepherd of the sheep, and ratified an eternal covenant with his blood—may he equip you with all you need for doing his will. May he produce in you, through the power of Jesus Christ, every good thing that is pleasing to him. All glory to him forever and ever! Amen." (Hebrews 13:20–21 NLT)

Meditations and Journaling:

Remember a time when you were disciplined by the Lord. Look back over your attitude and response to His discipline. How do you respond to His discipline? How have you responded to that issue in your life since that time?

Angels with Us

Do not forget to entertain strangers, for by so doing some have unwittingly entertained angels.

HEBREWS 13:2

The way God continually cares for His children reminds me of the depth of His love. In ways seen and unseen, we are cared for and protected. His love surrounds us when we do not feel loved, when we do not feel worthy of His love. One of the unseen forms of protection and provision that we do not often consider is the ministry of angels that surround us. Scripture reminds us that there is another realm inhabited by angelic forces, good and evil, and our lives are impacted on earth by what is happening in that heavenly unseen realm. Job's life was deeply impacted by what happened in the unseen realm (Job 1:6–12). We too, may experience joys and trials that have no origin on earth. Our call is to trust God in our circumstances and know that He sees all and is over all and will <u>never</u> allow His children to be tested beyond what they can endure. He created you, and He knows your limits and His purposes for your life.

Believers in Jesus Christ are often aided in this earthly life by angels. Speaking of angels, the writer of Hebrews calls them ministering spirits. "Are they not all ministering spirits sent out to serve for the sake of those who are to inherit salvation?" (Hebrews 1:14 ESV). Our culture is awash in myths and beliefs about angels that do not correspond with scripture, resulting in worship of angels. Sometimes these beliefs have crept into the church. We can take away three things from the scripture in Hebrews: (1) angels are spirits, part of the heavenly unseen realm; (2) they are 'sent out' by God as messengers of God, and (3) they are sent out to serve those who are to inherit salvation, believers in Christ. (Hebrews 1:14)

Additionally, scripture lets us know that angels are created beings, offering worship only to the Creator (Isaiah 6:1–4; Colossians 1:16). Satan is a created being, a fallen angel, who chose to challenge God for His glory and was condemned and thrown to earth with one-third of the angelic realm who followed him in his challenge (Isaiah 14:12–17). These fallen angels are called demons and there are wars in the unseen realm between God's angels and the demons. These unseen battles sometimes impact our lives. It is probably best that only God knows the intent and intensity of these spiritual battles. He has already won on our behalf.

Although God's children may be impacted by battles happening in the unseen realm, they are never uncovered from the love of God. His love is always active on our behalf. He sends out His messengers to provide protection. Angels minister to the saints for specific kingdom purposes, working in cooperation with the will of God, at the direction of God. It is not for us to know where and when God will deploy His angels in our lives, but we can trust that the angels assigned to us will act at His direction on our behalf.

The prayers of believers move God to respond and He sometimes sends His angels. Keep praying. When Elisha was sought by the King of Syria, Elisha's servant was afraid when he looked out and saw all of the king's chariots surrounding the place where they were. Elisha told him not to fear. "He said, "Do not be afraid, for those who are with us are more than those who are with them." Then Elisha prayed and said, "O Lord, please open his eyes that he may see." So the Lord opened the eyes of the young man, and he saw, and behold, the mountain was full of horses and chariots of fire all around Elisha" (2 Kings 6:16–17 ESV). You do not see the demonic forces targeting and surrounding you, but know that God's angelic forces surround you and are more than enough.

Believers have help to walk this life. We have the indwelling of God's Holy Spirit, angels watching over us and the intercession of Jesus on our behalf (Romans 8:34). Do not fear. Let your prayers open your eyes to all that God is doing in your life and know that He will rescue His children by any means necessary. Open your spiritual eyes and see the deliverance of the God who loves you more than you can imagine.

* * *

Time in His Word:

Read 2 Kings 6:8–23; Revelation 4:8;

Prayer:

Lord Jehovah, help us not to live in a spirit of fear and trepidation. Help us to live with all-out joy, trusting in You for every day, every situation. Thank You Father for Your love, Your protection and Your provision. May we read Your word and hold onto the assurance that You give us with each page. Let that assurance dwell deep in our spirits. We love You Father. In the name of Jesus Christ. Amen.

Meditations and Journaling:

What have you been taught and believed about angels? Can you identify some false beliefs about angels that you've been exposed to? Have you had experiences you believe to be angelic? Do those experiences correspond to the truth of scripture and the character of God?

Born of the Spirit

"I will be a Father to you, And you shall be My
sons and daughters, Says the Lord Almighty."

2 CORINTHIANS 6:18

Our struggles for identity take many forms. Sometimes we struggle because of race, ethnicity, sexual orientation, personality persuasion or birth order. Whatever the issue, at its core, the issue is one of longing to belong, to know that "I fit" or "I belong." We all need the inclusion and security of family and knowing that we are loved despite our flaws. Some may go a whole lifetime not belonging to a family, or not really feeling like that is the exact place where they are loved, wanted and needed.

At the moment you placed your faith in Jesus as Savior, you become a part of God's family. You are adopted by the Father who has always loved you, who has sought you and waited patiently for you to say yes to His entreaties. He made you. He knows everything about you, everything you've ever done, said or thought. He sees you as righteous because of the finished work of Jesus on the cross. God loves you and wants you to be a part of His family. You are chosen by God. "God decided in advance to adopt us into his own family by bringing us to himself through Jesus Christ. This is what he wanted to do, and it gave him great pleasure." (Ephesians 1:5 NLT) You are now overflowing with family, you have your earthly (natural) family – the one you were born into, and you have your spiritual family, the one you became a part of by God's grace.

You have been born again into a new family. In John 3, Jesus speaks to Nicodemus of being born again. This teacher of the Jews was confused when Jesus said that in order to see the kingdom of God you must be born again. Jesus then explained to him that there was a natural birth, of water, and a birth of the Spirit. It is this spiritual birth that brings you into God's family. Scripture says you are now called brothers (and sisters) of Jesus, joint heirs with Him in the kingdom. (Romans 8:17) This heirship allows us to partake in the blessings of the kingdom without question. Jesus Himself calls us brothers and sisters. "So now Jesus and the ones he makes holy have the same Father. That is why Jesus is not ashamed to call them his brothers and sisters" (Hebrews 2:11 NLT).

Many people have spent their lives in family situations that were threatening and/or full of upheaval. The blessing of belonging to God's family is the confidence we can have in the character of our heavenly Father. He will never disinherit us. He will never put us out of His family. He will always love us, even when we mess up. We never have to struggle again over identity issues – we know who we are. We are children of the King, blessed and holy, mercifully called and forgiven. There is security in being His. We are born of God (John 1:12). By His grace we have been grafted into the family of God and called children of Abraham, the father of faith.

This opportunity is available to all who choose Jesus as Lord. As far back as the Old Testament, God sought those who did not believe in Him and looked forward to a time when they too would believe. Concerning the Gentiles, God says in the prophecy of Hosea, "Then I will say to *those who were* not My people, 'You *are* My people!' And they shall say, '*You are* my God!' " (Hosea 2:23).

* * *

Time in His Word:

Read Isaiah 43:1; Galatians 4:4–7; Ephesians 2:19; Philippians 2:15–16

Prayer:

Abba Father, we bow to You, we praise You. We thank You for calling us into Your family. "I will bless the Lord at all times; his praise shall continually be in my mouth. My soul makes its boast in the Lord; let the humble hear and be glad. Oh, magnify the Lord with me, and let us exalt his name together! I sought the Lord, and he answered me and delivered me from all my fears." (Psalms 34:1–4 ESV) In the name of Jesus Christ. Amen.

Meditations and Journaling:

You never have to question your identity again. You are a child of the King. What identity issues have you had in your life? How has your walk with Christ helped you to let those go?

DAY 30

Reconciliation

And all of this is a gift from God, who brought us back to himself through Christ. And God has given us this task of reconciling people to him. For God was in Christ, reconciling the world to himself, no longer counting people's sins against them. And he gave us this wonderful message of reconciliation.

2 CORINTHIANS 5:18–19 NLT

Before you became a child of God through faith in Jesus, you were an enemy of God.

Our only hope of reconciliation to God is through Christ Jesus. The sacrifices of bulls and goats as practiced in the Old Testament served as only a temporary atonement for sins. Those sacrifices needed to be done over and over and they were only a picture of the perfect sacrifice to come in Jesus. We had no way out of our sin. Ephesians pictures us before Christ as being 'without hope, aliens to God's people and strangers to the promises of God' (Ephesians 2:12).

Jesus' death on the cross made atonement to God for our sins and allowed us to be reconciled to the Father. We are reconciled to the Father because we no longer carry the stink of sin on us, instead we carry the righteousness of Jesus. At the cross, Jesus substituted His righteousness for our sin. This atonement was for all time and only needed to be offered once. He rose from the dead, picturing our resurrection and power over death. We must praise God because we are free from the power of sin, and because we will never again be considered an enemy of God. We can never be separated from God. Our bodies will die but out soul is forever in His presence. God has innumerable gifts for His children.

We are not to be selfish with the gifts that God bestows on us. We have been reconciled to God through the blood of Jesus, but we have also been given the ministry of reconciliation. This means that each believer has the ability and responsibility to tell others how to be reconciled to God (2 Corinthians 5:18–20). I believe this to be more than a suggestion. The Great Commission commands us to "Go therefore and make disciples of all the nations, baptizing them in the name of the Father and of the Son and of the Holy Spirit" (Matthew 28:19). We are commanded to share the good news of reconciliation to God with others. This sharing does not require you to be a minister or a skilled orator. What is required is that you be willing to share with someone else what God has done in you, in your life.

God is a God of relationship. His ministry of reconciliation extends to how we live in relationships. He has done this work of reconciliation in us for others to see. We are called by him to love others, to even love our enemies. We are called to be reconciled first to our brothers (Matthew 5:24). In His death, Jesus reconciled the Jews and Gentiles, offering them one message of hope, and presenting them to God as one nation, dispensing with the previous division between the two (Ephesians 2:14–18).

In this ministry of reconciliation, we are reconciling broken relationships in our lives, but also showing Christ to others and providing them the opportunity to become reconciled to God and to others. What we do and how we live brings glory (or not) to our heavenly Father. In a world as broken as ours, this message of reconciliation is desperately needed. "Let your light so shine before men, that they may see your good works and glorify your Father in heaven" (Matthew 5:16).

* * *

Time in His Word:

Read Romans 5:10–11; 2 Corinthians 5:18–21; Ephesians 2:14–18, 4:32

Prayer:

Dear Father, I thank You first of all for reconciling me to Yourself; for calling me home. Thank You. Help me to live in such a way that I can draw others to You. Help me to be an element in reconciling the broken relationships around me; those relationships in my home, my family, my church and in people I meet. Feed me Your words Father, I open my mouth to receive, my ears to hear and my heart to live it out. Let me not be an instrument of discord that causes disharmony. Lord, Your reconciliation is needed this day, Father, this hour. Help me to be Your instrument. In the name of Jesus Christ. Amen.

Meditations and Journaling:

In your life, where is reconciliation needed? Write out your prayer to God asking for His help in making reconciliation happen. Ask God to reveal to you someone who needs to hear the message of the gospel and be reconciled to God. Prepare to be obedient in sharing the gospel with them.

DAY 31

Regeneration

Therefore, if anyone is in Christ, he is a
new creation; old things have passed away;
behold, all things have become new.

2 CORINTHIANS 5:17

I picture the moment of salvation very much like the events described in the parable of the prodigal son (Luke 15:11–32). The son chooses to leave home. After leaving, he spends his fortune doing whatever he wants, until a moment occurs when he finds himself in desperate need. He decides to return home to the Father who loves him and who will tenderly care for him. Scripture says "the son came to his senses." He came to his senses and headed home. His father saw him coming and ran to embrace him, having compassion on him. The father put a ring, a robe, and sandals on him. They killed the fatted calf and there was a celebration to welcome the son home. The son was reconciled to his father.

Like the rebellious son, there is a day when we come to our senses and choose to ask Jesus Christ to be Lord of our lives. On that day, angels in heaven celebrate (Luke 15:10). At the moment of belief, the believer is indwelt with the Holy Spirit, spiritual gifts are given to the believer, and they are welcomed into the family of God. There is more that happens at salvation, much more. When you are adopted into God's family you become a new creation. This does not mean a refurbishing of the old person; it means God literally making you into a <u>new</u>, spirit-filled man. This is regeneration, being made new by God.

In your old life, pre-Jesus, you were considered dead, but now you are made alive (Ephesians 2:1). This 'new creation' does not refer to a new physical body, but a new inward man. At the moment of salvation, you are given the Spirit of God and you become a spiritual creature. This is new in that where you previously responded to the world based only on your physical nature, you now will relate based on the new spiritual presence of God living in you. No longer just a physical creature, you are now a spiritual creature, able to respond to God in spirit and in truth (John 4:23). Based on this new you, you will respond to sin and to life in a different way. You will pray and worship God in accordance with the Spirit residing in you. With your Spirit you will glorify Jesus Christ, the lamb crucified for your redemption.

Baptism is a picture of the death, burial and resurrection of Jesus, by whom we have obtained salvation. It also presents a picture of what happens at our salvation. Your old life of sin is buried (immersion) and you are raised to new life in Jesus, with Jesus. Ephesians depicts our changed life as 'taking off' the old man and 'putting on' the new man – the new creation that you are (Ephesians 4:23-24). Although God's Spirit now resides in you, you still have free will to respond to life. God's encouragement to us, through scripture, is that we grow in knowledge and walk according to His Spirit as we now respond to life. We are told to walk in this 'newness of life' (Romans 6:4). Scripture encourages us to immerse ourselves in the Word of God and allow the word to transform our minds so that we respond to the world based on our new Spirit nature rather than our old fleshly nature. (Romans 12:2) As we grow in learning God's word, responding to the world based on that word should become our new normal – we are being transformed.

The old you, able to operate only based on your flesh, no longer exists. The new you is hidden in Christ, protected and cared for by our holy God who is your security in this world (Colossians 3:3). There may be times when you doubt this regeneration, times when you become discouraged by your response to life, but the Holy Spirit living in you testifies and confirms to you that you belong to God. "For all who are led by the Spirit of God are children of God" (Romans 8:14 NLT). Allow His Spirit to lead and be amazed at the changes you will see as you grow.

* * *

Time in His Word:

Read Romans 6:4–14; Romans 8:9–11; Colossians 3:3

Prayer:

Heavenly Father, I am a new creature. Your word says so, and I believe Your word. Lord, there are times and days when the old me surfaces and I don't much feel like a new creature. Help me Father to walk in the newness of life and to respond, not according to how I feel, but according to Your truth. Help me to live this life as Your new creature. I thank You now Father for the changes You will work in me. In the name of Jesus Christ. Amen

Meditations and Journaling:

How have you changed since accepting Jesus Christ as Savior? Think of at least one specific way that your response to life is new.

For God so loved the world that He gave His only begotten Son, that whoever believes in Him should not perish but have everlasting life. For God did not send His Son into the world to condemn the world, but that the world through Him might be saved.

JOHN 3:16–17

Chapter 4
ETERNAL LOVE

Learning outcomes for chapter 4 (Days 32 – to the end)

- ✓ Understand the absolute security of God's love into eternity
- ✓ Understand the mission of redemption through the eyes of Jesus
- ✓ Understand our part in this salvation
- ✓ Recognize and respond to your opportunity to choose whether you will experience His eternal love.
- ✓ Do not let today be your stumbling block

DAY 32

His Holy Word

Now we have received not the spirit of the world,
but the Spirit who is from God, that we might
understand the things freely given us by God.

1 CORINTHIANS 2:12 ESV

God's desire from before Genesis has been to restore His people to a state of perfection living in perfect relationship with Him. Every gift given to His children leads toward those purposes, restoration and reconciliation. Each gift is perfect, designed for His children to know His heart of love for each of them.

God's holy word, the Bible, aligns with every other gift that He has given us to help us understand His heart toward us. His word helps us to know His character, understand how to live godly, align our character with His and to be able to share with others Who we know and what we know. In His word we learn from the examples of others how God desires us to live. As you read the Bible, the Holy Spirit teaches you and guides you into a correct understanding. Later, the Spirit will bring these things you have learned to your mind when you need them.

The gift of the Holy Spirit leading us into understanding is not insignificant. Many people have said "I read the Bible, and I just don't get it!" They don't get it because scripture is divinely inspired and intended for the mind inhabited by His Spirit. "But people who aren't spiritual can't receive these truths from God's Spirit. It all sounds foolish to them and they can't understand it, for only those who are spiritual can understand what the Spirit means" (1 Corinthians 2:14 NLT).

Scripture was written for us, as lessons and examples of ways to live, and also as ways not to live. Scripture does not present a fairy tale vision of God's people, but rather we see the raw truth about our own character as we look into scripture. We see that Moses and David were murderers, Aaron allowed idol worship, Adam followed Eve rather than God's instructions, we see Elijah huddled in shame after being threatened by Jezebel, John the Baptist questioning whether Jesus was the promised Messiah, and Peter denying Jesus. These are not pretty pictures, but this is who we are in our most human moments.

Scripture also lets us see transformed lives and the character of God. It is in knowing the character of God that we can have hope and understand how to extend His mercy and compassion to others. We look in scripture and see how God was able to use Moses, David, Aaron, Elijah and Peter despite their human failings. We see the redemption of Adam's seed and the tenderness of Jesus toward John the Baptist and Peter. Scripture shows us God's character and how He will use fallible men and women who are sold out to him. He will use imperfect people who are faithful and available to Him.

Scripture is about the character of God toward man. It is a gift in sixty-six parts, each part imparting His love in a different way. It was written for our learning, "that we through the patience and comfort of the Scriptures might have hope" (Romans 15:4–6). We need this hope because sometimes we fail as we strive to be godly. We despair of ever getting it right. We need this hope because when we fall, we believe the lie that surely God could not forgive us this time. We need this hope in order to know the character of God; to know that 'yes, even this time,' His mercy and grace prevail. God gives us this hope in His word as a sure and steadfast anchor for our souls (Hebrews 6:19), holding us fast to the truth of God's words so that we can live godly and bring Him glory in this life and in the life to come.

* * *

Time in His Word:

Read 1 Corinthians 2:9-16; 1 Timothy 4:13; 2 Timothy 2:15–26

Prayer:

Our Father in heaven, thank You for the many gifts that You shower us with. Thank You for the abundance of Your word, leading us, guiding us, correcting us, convicting us. Your word, Father is all things to us. Help us to heed Your commands and understand Your precepts. We know that You have given us everything in Your word for us to live godly lives and bring You glory in this life. Help us to take full advantage of Your word to walk in all Your ways. Forgive us Father when we do not take time for Your word, and lead us back, knowing that it is life and breath to each one of Your children and we need it daily. In the name of Jesus Christ. Amen.

Meditations and Journaling:

Meditate on your habits of Bible study and reading. Technology offers us many more ways to spend time in the word than we had in the past. Are you taking advantage of the many available opportunities to know God better through His word? What is your most common excuse for not being in the word? Pray about that, ask for guidance to overcome that mindset.

DAY 33
Absolute Security

"For I am the Lord, I do not change; Therefore
you are not consumed, O sons of Jacob.

We live in perilous times. Our times are not perilous just because everyone is strapped and ready to shoot, but because people are hopeless and searching. In their searching, they have come up with their own answers to life instead of seeking God's truth. In their hopelessness they live just for today, seeing no reason to aspire to faithfulness and righteousness. There is no regard for life because they have no reason to live for tomorrow. For the ones living without hope, if tomorrow comes, it will just be another day.

The prophet Malachi and John the Baptist came in similar times, many years apart. Both came at a time when people had become comfortable with their rituals. Malachi came to the Israelite people who had returned from captivity but never turned completely back to God. The city was rebuilt, the temple was complete, but the people lacked faith. They had given up on seeing the fulfillment of God's covenants with Abraham and David. God sent Malachi the prophet to turn them back to God but his exhortations to them fell on deaf ears. Every accusation from God about their faithlessness was met with a question designed to justify their position before God. God reminded them of His love for them, and they respond with "In what way have you loved us?" (Malachi 1:2). The conversation continues like that until God presents them with a picture of judgment in Malachi chapter 4. Even then, God invites them back into covenant relationship with Him and reminds them of His love for them.

Likewise, John the Baptist came preaching repentance and foretelling

LOVE MAGNIFIED   103

the coming of the Messiah. He was met with a culture entrenched in their own righteousness. The Jewish community had designed a culture of rituals and traditions that went beyond the law given by Moses from God. They were zealous and righteous in their own stead. Their religious system had taken precedence over God's truth. Those religious scholars who scrupulously studied the Old Testament denied every sign that showed them Jesus was the promised Messiah. John called those who came to him for the baptism of repentance a brood of vipers. He warned them of coming judgment, saying "Even now the ax of God's judgment is poised, ready to sever the roots of the trees. Yes, every tree that does not produce good fruit will be chopped down and thrown into the fire" (Luke 3:9 NLT). And yet, despite their hardened hearts, Jesus came to offer them salvation.

In our time, in the time of Malachi, and in the time of Jesus and John the Baptist, we can be lulled into feeling there is no payback for the effort required to live a righteous life. Our culture has pushed aside the Word of God, settling instead for individual truth and relativism. In this environment it becomes easy to disregard the signs of coming judgment because few know the truth from God's word. But, from the beginning of time there is a constant that we must understand. God says "I change not" (Malachi 3:6).

This is the absolute security we have for today. The same God is over all times. His message of love does not change. His promise of hope and redemption does not change. His promised eternity does not change. His judgment of wrong, and the purveyor of wrong, does not change. He is God today, tomorrow and always – the God of past, present and future, the God I AM. He is the only unchanging part of life – whether you are a believer or not. For the believer, this truth is our absolute security and bulwark against the hopelessness of the times we live in. The truth of who God is will not change for the one who denies Christ - this is the truth they will know for certain in judgment.

Because of God's unchanging character we are not consumed over our sin. Because God does not change, we have a blessed assurance that the sure salvation Jesus offers to everyone is true. Because He does not change, He loves us every day, no less on the days we mess up. He is God, He does not change. That is absolute security for believers.

* * *

Time in His Word:

Read Psalm 146:5–6; Malachi chapters 1 and 4; Luke 3:1–17

Prayer:

Lord Jehovah You are our hiding place in all times. You are our hope, our constant standard for righteousness and our security. You are the great I AM. Help us to remember each day that You do not change. Your precepts and statutes do not change, and Your ways do not change. Mostly, Father, help us to remember that Your love for Your children does not change – we desperately need to bask in that truth. We bless You, honor You and praise Your name through the mighty name of our Savior, Jesus Christ. Amen.

Meditations and Journaling:

What are you resting in today? Where is your security? Make an assessment and talk to God about what you find.

DAY 34
An Issue of Obedience

*Keep your heart with all diligence, For
out of it spring the issues of life.*

PROVERBS 4:23

Each of us inherited our sin nature from Adam (Romans 5:12). God says the penalty for sin is death (Romans 6:23). We are all doomed to death everlasting without an atonement for our sin. Without the shedding of blood, there would be no atonement for sin (Hebrews 9:22). Because of His love for us, God sent His Son Jesus to shed His blood and die to pay the sin debt that we owe. Jesus was the only perfect and holy sacrifice, the only sacrifice acceptable to God. Those who choose to accept this free gift of salvation are forgiven of their sins and made righteous in the sight of God (1 John 2:2; Ephesians 1:7). Because of God's love demonstrated in Jesus, and the atoning sacrifice of Jesus, believers are forgiven for all sins, past, present and future.

This forgiveness does not mean we will never sin again, it means we have an advocate with the Father (Jesus) who intercedes with the Father when we repent of sin and ask forgiveness (1 John 2:1–2). Because of our advocate, we are declared righteous. This sin debt is not a debt we can repay. We are broke and empty; we have nothing to pay that debt with. Our forgiveness cost Jesus death by crucifixion. Just as we have been forgiven, we are commanded to forgive others. While we could not pay the sin debt, forgiving others is something we can do.

Forgiveness is not easy, but with the Helper coming alongside, we can forgive others in order to receive the blessings of restored fellowship and forgiveness for our ongoing sins. Scripture says that if we do not forgive others, God will not forgive us. "If you forgive those who sin against you, your heavenly Father will forgive you. But if you refuse to forgive others, your Father will not forgive your sins" (Matthew 6:14–15 NLT). Scripture adds the additional commandment that we forgive "from the heart" (Matthew 18:35). Our forgiveness cannot be just dutiful words; it must be sincere. God knows out hearts; He knows the difference. In fact, we know the difference.

In a short book of the New Testament, Philemon, we meet a slave named Onesimus. Onesimus has stolen something (money?) and run away from his master, Philemon, in Colosse. Onesimus runs to Rome where he providentially meets Paul and becomes a Christian. As Paul gets to know Onesimus he realizes that he knows his master, Philemon. Years before meeting Onesimus, Paul led Philemon to Christ. The church at Colosse meets in Philemon's home. Scripture does not tell us how Paul met Onesimus, only that Onesimus was very useful to Paul in his imprisonment, and that Paul was very fond of him. Paul wrote a letter to Philemon, telling him about these circumstances and explaining that he intended to send Onesimus back to him. This is not a commentary about slavery. It is a commentary about the forgiveness that must exist in the heart of brothers and sisters in Christ.

Several situations needed to be resolved. Now that he knew the situation, Paul had no right to Onesimus' services without the permission of Philemon. As a new Christian, Onesimus had a different Spirit living in him now and he had an obligation to do the right thing by his brother Philemon, including restitution for what he stole. Philemon had to search his heart, forgive Onesimus, and receive him back as a brother in Christ – a different relationship than they had before. Paul offered to be responsible for the restitution, but the situations still involved matters of the heart and would not be easy to resolve. That is the nature of forgiveness - it is difficult and involves our heart, but it is still commanded. We must guard our hearts against the tendency to be unforgiving. We must guard our hearts against the desire to seek vengeance when we feel we have been wronged.

We do not know the outcome of the Paul/Onesimus/Philemon situation, but each one of us has a situation in our life that demands forgiveness, from the heart. Jesus came to die for our sins, so we could be forgiven. Day by day, hour by hour, he walked steadily toward the cross, with divine knowledge of everything that would entail. Bleeding, on the cross, His thoughts were of forgiveness "Father, forgive them, for they don't know what they are doing" (Luke 23:34 NLT).

Forgiveness is the foundation of our faith. Can we offer any less as we live in the righteousness granted by His sacrifice for us?

* * *

Time in His Word:

Read Romans 3:23–25; Ephesians 4:32; Hebrews 12:14–15

Prayer:

Our Father in heaven, forgive us for our sins and cleanse us. Father create in us a heart that is tender and loving and obedient. Help us to abhor pride and arrogance, put it far away from us. Help us to humbly forgive those who sin against us; it is hard to do but not impossible. You have shown us that it is possible. Help us to walk in humility and meekness. We seek to have Your heart Father, to please You and to live at peace with all men. Give us a mindset to obey You rather than our own inclinations. Let us listen to Your truth when we are offended and respond as Your word teaches. Cleanse us of the old nature, transform us so we can love others in the same way You love us. Help us to be willing participants in the work You are doing in our hearts. Thank You for our forgiveness. In the name of Jesus Christ. Amen.

Meditations and Journaling:

Who do you need to forgive? Are there circumstances in your life that you are holding others responsible for? Do you need to forgive yourself for something? Ask God to help you remove the block in your spirit that keeps you hanging onto old hurts. Ask and allow Him to soothe and release you from the guilt, anger and hurt that blocks forgiveness and freedom.

DAY 35

Understanding the Mission

*"Now My soul is troubled, and what shall I
say? 'Father, save Me from this hour'? But
for this purpose I came to this hour.*

JOHN 12:27

Experienced hikers are not caught off guard when the terrain they are on
shifts. One moment they are walking on a smooth path, then the terrain
shifts from smooth to rugged. They have to be prepared. Jesus knew the
terrain had shifted in His ministry. "Before the Passover celebration, Jesus
knew that his hour had come to leave this world and return to his Father.
He had loved his disciples during his ministry on earth, and now he loved
them to the very end" (John 13:1 NLT).

Jesus had maintained a distance from Jerusalem in the last weeks of
His active ministry, but as the Passover approached, He set His face toward
Jerusalem because He knew that was where His destiny led and prophecy
had to be fulfilled. He looked beyond the cross to His future glory with the
Father. He directed His disciples to prepare for the Passover celebration,
their last supper together. He would accomplish several things with them
that evening as they had this last time together.

During this last time together, Jesus told them frankly what would
happen to Him; "You know that after two days is the Passover, and the
Son of Man will be delivered up to be crucified" (Matthew 26:2). He told
them He would be betrayed by one of the twelve (Matthew 26:21). He
told them very bluntly that He would not be with them much longer and
that they would face tribulation in their world; "They will put you out of
the synagogues; yes, the time is coming that whoever kills you will think

that he offers God service" (John 16:2). He didn't leave anyone out, He said they all would scatter, they all would stumble because of the coming events. Jesus knew their faith. He was preparing them for the truth of hostile times to come, but He was not implementing a militia or initiating a military takeover as some had expected the Messiah to do (Luke 24:21).

Jesus reminded them of His mission; He came to save the world. He gave them an example of service, washing their feet, symbolizing their spiritual cleansing and union with Him, reminding them to carry that union forward to others. He instituted the Lord's Supper, communion, telling them to "Do this in remembrance of me" (Luke 22:19). Jesus then gave them one final command, to love one another. "By this all will know that you are My disciples, if you have love for one another" (John 13:35). His love in them, visible to the world as they loved one another and remained in unity would be the hallmark of His mission and the unifying factor that would remind them of Him and hold them together.

That night there was a lot to take in. They were sorrowful, but not hopeless. It was a full night. After their supper, events moved quickly and forcefully, perhaps the reason they didn't seem to remember two important statements made by Jesus: (1) "after I am raised" and (2) "I will go ahead of you to Galilee" (Matthew 26:32). It was a promised meeting in Galilee, but after His death they were sorrowful and wondering, remaining in Jerusalem, not remembering the promised resurrection.

They did not go to Galilee, but He met them where they were. He will meet you where you are.

* * *

Time in His Word:

Read Matthew 26; John 12–13

Prayer:

Lord, prepare us for the times to come because only You know what is ahead. Help us remember You are always with us. Prepare us for the attacks of Satan to come. Strengthen us, comfort us, open our eyes to Your word so that we may see truth. Help us prepare in Your word for the battle to come, that we will stand and see Your victory. Strengthen us and help us to love one another so we are a testimony of You to the world around us. Let us spread Your love abroad to others. In the name of Jesus Christ. Amen.

Meditations and Journaling:

God will meet you where you are. Where are you today? What circumstances challenge you? Call on His name, expecting His mercy, His wisdom, His riches, His grace and His love to overflow you and your circumstances. Believe that He will meet you right where you are and address your needs.

DAY 36

In the Garden

When Jesus had spoken these words, He went out
with His disciples over the Brook Kidron, where
there was a garden, which He and His disciples
entered. And Judas, who betrayed Him, also knew the
place; for Jesus often met there with His disciples.

JOHN 18:1–2

Step-by -step, Jesus comes closer to the cross. In His humanity, He wished that hour could pass from Him. "Now My soul is troubled, and what shall I say? 'Father, save Me from this hour'? But for this purpose I came to this hour" (John 12:27). He nears His purpose of redeeming mankind, but also knows that in His coming crucifixion He casts down the one whose head He was called to bruise. "The time for judging this world has come, when Satan, the ruler of this world, will be cast out" (John 12:31 NLT). His death and resurrection will conquer death and defeat Satan for all time. His divine mission would be accomplished on earth as it is in heaven.

Jesus and His disciples left the upper room and went to the Mount of Olives, to the garden of Gethsemane. He took Peter, James and John with Him away from the others, asking them to watch and pray. He went a distance away from them. As always, He sought His Father in prayer. His soul was troubled and He submitted Himself fully to His Father. Three times He prayed and three times He fully submitted His will to His Father. "Father, if you are willing, please take this cup of suffering away from me. Yet I want your will to be done, not mine" (Luke

22:42 NLT). Jesus never second-guessed His mission, His purpose, His final completion of redemption, or His defeat of Satan. He was fully committed, all in.

Each time He returned to the three, He found them sleeping, not mindful of the coming persecutions. After His warnings to them in the Upper Room, He is urging them to be watchful and to pray for strength for the coming times. Now they were out of time. The time had come for Satan to attempt the final action that he assumed would give him victory. Satan is not omniscient; he does not know the plans of God. He is a created being, subject to the sovereignty of Jehovah Almighty and not privileged to know the end of all things. He does, however, know his end and the end of those demons he rules, so he strives to do whatever he can to convert many to his side and ruin the testimony of believers.

Judas Iscariot's moment had come. He came to the garden to arrest Jesus with a detachment of troops given to him by the chief priest and scribes. His pre-arranged signal was a kiss. He attempted to kiss Jesus, "But Jesus said to him, 'Judas, are you betraying the Son of Man with a kiss?'" (Luke 22:48). The disciples thought this was the moment to act. Peter pulled his sword and cut off the right ear of the servant of the high priest. Jesus said to His disciples, "'Permit even this.' And He touched his ear and healed him" (Luke 22:51). Jesus then allowed Himself to be taken away, acknowledging the power of darkness in that hour brought on by the evil living in the hearts of men because of Satan (Luke 22:53), but knowing the sure victory of the God of heaven.

Scripture says all the disciples forsook him (Matthew 25:56). One by one, those eleven disciples who had vowed during the last supper to stand by Him, left Him. Their leaving fulfilled the prophecy spoken in Zechariah 13:7: "Strike the Shepherd, And the sheep will be scattered."

There are moments when you assume it can't get any worse. And then it does. Peter and another disciple followed as they took Jesus to the house of the High Priest, Caiaphas for trial.

* * *

Time in His Word:

Read Mark 14

Prayer:

Lord, Your word says the battles we fight are not against flesh and blood, but against the rulers, against the authorities, against the cosmic powers over this present darkness, against the spiritual forces of evil in the heavenly places. Help us to remember that You have promised to fight our battles. Help us to stand and watch Your deliverance. Remind us always Father that the battle is Yours, and that the battle is already won. Let us stand in Your presence and win because of You. Remind us that Satan always seeks to harm us. Help us not to faint when he comes calling, but to trust in Your power and might and not our own. Grant us Your peace in the battle; may we submit to Your authority and not fret or live in a spirit of fear. In the name of Jesus Christ. Amen.

Meditations and Journaling:

Jesus, our high priest, experienced every circumstance we can imagine, including betrayal, yet He was sinless. Examine how you have handled betrayal in the past. Has your response to betrayal changed? How does knowing betrayal is a spiritual battle allow you to change your perception and response?

DAY 37
Judas Iscariot

*The Son of Man indeed goes just as it is written
of Him, but woe to that man by whom the Son
of Man is betrayed! It would have been good
for that man if he had not been born."*

MATTHEW 26:24

It may not seem like there is much to learn from the life of Judas Iscariot, but everything in the Bible is written for our edification, therefore, we should look at the life of Judas and discern what will help us grow.

Judas was one of the twelve disciples chosen by Jesus (Matthew 10:4). His character was evident from the beginning. Jesus recognized him as a devil (John 6:70–71) and called him the son of perdition (John 17:12), implying his destiny of eternal damnation. Judas was the group treasurer. He stole from the money bag (John 12:6). Knowing that the chief priests and scribes were seeking to kill Jesus, Judas went voluntarily to them, seeking to betray Jesus. "Then Judas Iscariot, one of the twelve, went to the chief priests to betray Him to them. And when they heard it, they were glad, and promised to give him money. So he sought how he might conveniently betray Him" (Mark 14:10–11).

Judas betrayed Jesus for thirty pieces of silver. From the time he received the money, he was always on the lookout for an opportunity to betray Him (Matthew 26:14–16). On the night of the last supper, Satan entered into Judas and he carried out his plan of betrayal (John 13:27). After Jesus was judged to be guilty and sentenced to crucifixion, Judas had an attack of conscience and attempted to return the money, saying, "I have sinned by betraying innocent blood." The chief priests and scribes refused to grant him absolution by taking back the money. They told him to handle his own conscience. Judas then committed suicide (Matthew 27:3–10).

Scripture tells us clearly that the events of Jesus' life from birth to ascension were prophesied many years before. In fact, there were times when Jesus deliberately took an action to fulfill scripture. This happened when He came to John the Baptist to be baptized and John objected, saying Jesus ought to be baptizing him. "Jesus answered him, 'Let it be so now, for thus it is fitting for us to fulfill all righteousness.' Then he consented" (Matthew 3:15 ESV). Judas' actions were in fulfillment of scripture, but were never an excuse for unrighteousness. God does not call anyone to sin, or cause them to sin. God can sovereignly use whoever He chooses, knowing that person's disposition.

Judas' heart was fertile ground for Satan. Judas walked with Jesus and the other eleven disciples for three years. Never once was his heart tender toward the gospel, leading to repentance. "He who is of God hears God's words; therefore you do not hear, because you are not of God" (John 8:47). When he felt remorse for his actions of betrayal, he did not turn to God in repentance, instead he went to the scribes and then killed himself. This is important because, as believers, we need to know that there will be those who will always have a hard heart toward God and may never repent. Our right course of action is not judgment, because only God can judge the heart. We can never presume to know the outcome of a person's life or make a judgment about who we share the gospel with. Our right course of action is to continue planting seeds and loving as God loved, praying and preparing for the miracle of salvation. Always leave room for the Holy Spirit to work.

In the parable of the wheat and the tares (Matthew 13:24–43), a farmer plants good wheat but when the crop comes up there are tares intermingled in the field. Tares are a similar looking plant, only able to be distinguished at maturity. When asked about the tares, the farmer says an enemy has planted them. He says not to try to take the tares out until harvest when they are distinguishable and can be burned. This is a picture of the kingdom of God, where Satan the enemy has planted his children in with God's children, causing deception and discord. The harvest pictures the end of the age when the angels will separate the wheat from the tares and burn the tares. "Therefore as the tares are gathered and burned in the fire, so it will be at the end of this age. The Son of Man will send out His angels, and they will gather out of His kingdom all things that offend, and those who practice lawlessness, and will cast them into the furnace of fire" (Matthew 13:40–42).

Jesus will judge at the end of the age; judgment is not our job. We should always know we are in a spiritual battle with angels and demons surrounding us. We should always know that Satan seeks to steal, kill and destroy (John 10:10). We must remain vigilant and discerning and obedient to the Word of God. Greater is He that is in you than he that is in the world (1 John 4:4).

* * *

Time in His Word:

Read John 8:42–47; John 13:24–30

Prayer:

Lord, help us to be vigilant and obedient every day. Remind us always that judgment is not our job. We desire to grow closer to You and know Your character so we will never be disarmed by the tactics of the enemy. Lead us to share Your truth with everyone who will hear. In the name of Jesus Christ. Amen.

Meditations and Journaling:

What do you casually say and think about the devil? What do you hear others say? Know that he is your enemy, seeking to destroy your testimony. How do your words, thoughts and actions show disregard for the seriousness of the devil's intent toward you?

Healing the Opposition

*Beloved, do not avenge yourselves, but rather
give place to wrath; for it is written, "Vengeance
is Mine, I will repay," says the Lord.*

ROMANS 12:19

As they sat at the Last Supper, Jesus explained to His disciples what was to come. He explained the changing climate they would experience after His death. He advised them to prepare for these new times. "But now," he said, "take your money and a traveler's bag. And if you don't have a sword, sell your cloak and buy one! For the time has come for this prophecy about me to be fulfilled: 'He was counted among the rebels.' Yes, everything written about me by the prophets will come true" (Luke 22:36-37 NLT). Jesus was not advocating war or violence, simply warning them about what was to come and advising them to be prepared. He knew He would be counted as a rebel, and by association, they would too.

When Judas and his detachment of troops appeared in the garden to arrest Jesus, the environment appeared hostile and Peter immediately pulled his sword and cut off the ear of the servant of the high priest. Perhaps he misunderstood Jesus' directions? "But Jesus answered and said, 'Permit even this.' And He touched his ear and healed him" (Luke 22:51). Jesus healed the opposition, the one who came to arrest Him. Peter acted impetuously, but Jesus understood the necessity for events to play out as prophecy had foretold. This was not the time for a military take-over. Redemption for all mankind was at stake.

Jesus never compromised the foundational principles or the truth of His ministry. In healing the servant's ear, He was true to one of the first principles ever spoken by Him: love your enemy. "But I say to you, love your enemies, bless those who curse you, do good to those who hate you, and pray for those who spitefully use you and persecute you, that you may be sons of your Father in heaven; for He makes His sun rise on the evil and on the good, and sends rain on the just and on the unjust" (Matthew 5:44–45). When questioned by Pilate about His kingdom, Jesus explained why His disciples would not fight this battle with swords. Jesus answered, "My Kingdom is not an earthly kingdom. If it were, my followers would fight to keep me from being handed over to the Jewish leaders. But my Kingdom is not of this world" (John 18:36 NLT).

To be sons and daughters of our Father in heaven, we must learn how to operate in the world we live in according to the foundational principles of His kingdom. This sometimes presents a conflict because we must live in the world, without subscribing to the prevailing culture of the world. Love your enemies, leave vengeance to God. Like Peter, we will be tempted to draw our natural inclination into the battles and strike out. But we are admonished to fight our battles with love and prayer, always praying and allowing the Holy Spirit to lead.

Love your enemy – that's hard. Sometimes, like Jesus said to Peter, we have to "permit even this." There will be times when our most loving response is to overlook a comment or an action that we'd like to respond to, but love your enemy. The action or comment you overlook may lead to an opportunity to share the gospel. People will not understand your failure to respond. They don't have to understand as long as you do. Pray first. Understand that the love you extend to your enemy may bring healing in the long run because your actions will point them to your Father in heaven. That is where true healing resides.

* * *

Time in His Word:

Read Proverbs 25:21–22; Romans 12:19–21

Prayer:

Father, this is hard. We not only do not want to love our enemies; we do not want to see them healed. But Father, we want to honor You and we want to see Your word living in us and in everyone we meet. So, we lay down our will and ask You to create in us clean hearts that love Your truth more than we love our own vindication. Help us Father to grow to that place where we can generously love our enemies with our whole hearts as You tell us to. In the name of Jesus Christ. Amen.

Meditations and Journaling:

What enemy always makes you want to lash out? Dig deeper and try to understand why that one gets under your skin so easily. Then, pray for God's direction on the best way to love this enemy and point them to God. Ask God to heal the hurts that are revealed.

DAY 39
Looking Beyond

> *So the chief priests and the Pharisees gathered the*
> *Council and said, "What are we to do? For this man*
> *performs many signs. If we let him go on like this,*
> *everyone will believe in him, and the Romans will*
> *come and take away both our place and our nation."*
>
> JOHN 11:47–48 ESV

To preserve their own positions, the Jewish leaders wanted Jesus dead by any means necessary. They convinced themselves that He would be a sacrifice for the nation. "You don't realize that it's better for you that one man should die for the people than for the whole nation to be destroyed" (John 11:50 NLT). After His arrest in the garden Jesus was taken first to Annas, the father-in-law of Caiaphas the high priest, then to Caiaphas, then to Pilate, then to Herod, and finally back to Pilate. So much effort to find Him guilty and deserving of death. They tried to find witnesses who could accuse Him, but the witnesses couldn't agree. "Inside, the leading priests and the entire high council were trying to find evidence against Jesus, so they could put him to death. But they couldn't find any. Many false witnesses spoke against him, but they contradicted each other" (Mark 14:55–56 NLT).

While they debated, Peter stood near the door of the courtyard watching. One of the girls who brought him in asked him if he was one of Jesus' followers; Peter denied that he knew Him. Then again, as he stood near the fire warming himself, they asked if he was one of His disciples. Peter again denied knowing Jesus. Then, accused of being in the garden with Jesus, Peter, for the third time, denied knowing Him. Immediately a rooster crowed. "And the Lord turned and looked at Peter. And Peter remembered the word of the Lord, how He had said to him, "Before the rooster crows, you will deny Me three times" (Luke 22:61). Peter, who had just that evening boasted "I will never be made to stumble," went out and wept.

As Peter wept, Caiaphas sought harder to find grounds to put Jesus to death. He demanded of Jesus: "Tell us if You are the Christ, the Son of God!" Jesus said to him, "It is as you said. Nevertheless, I say to you, hereafter you will see the Son of Man sitting at the right hand of the Power, and coming on the clouds of heaven" (Matthew 26:63–64). Finally, Caiaphas had what he sought. He tore his clothes in a show of piety and proclaimed to everyone present: "He is guilty of blasphemy."

Events had moved fast up to that point, but now they went into overdrive. Jesus was taken to Pilate with the Jews assured of an immediate death sentence. After a visit to Herod and back to Pilate, and accusations to Pilate that Jesus threatened Caesar, Pilate finally caved to their demands for crucifixion, even after saying "I find no fault in Him." To preserve his place in society, Pilate gave in to the dictates of men rather than follow his conscience. He had Jesus scourged, released Barabbas, and presented Jesus for crucifixion, washing his hands of all guilt in the process.

In all this, Jesus made no defense on His own behalf. He came as a baby in a manger, God incarnate, to redeem His people from their sin. With infinite knowledge of what He would endure, Jesus walked steadily toward the cross. Redemption for mankind was His Father's will; He came to do the will of His Father.

The worst was yet to come. Jesus, our model in all things, looked beyond the cross to His return to heaven. Even before crucifixion, He was able to say to His Father in heaven: "Father, the hour has come. Glorify Your Son, that Your Son also may glorify You, as You have given Him authority over all flesh, that He should give eternal life to as many as You have given Him. And this is eternal life, that they may know You, the only true God, and Jesus Christ whom You have sent. I have glorified You on the earth. I have finished the work which You have given Me to do. And now, O Father, glorify Me together with Yourself, with the glory which I had with You before the world was" (John 17:1–5).

In your circumstances today, look beyond. Look beyond earth to see the final fulfillment of the promises of salvation.

* * *

Time in His Word:

Read Luke 22

Prayer:

Lord, You are our hope for today and tomorrow. Help us to focus beyond our circumstances of today to Your promised peace. Help us to remember that we want to live in such a way that we get to hear You say "Well done." Help us to remember that You fight our battles, that vengeance is Yours. Walk with us in the trenches and help us know that You are the ladder that pulls us out. Thank You Father for hope beyond these circumstances. In the name of Jesus Christ. Amen.

Meditations and Journaling:

Are there circumstances in your life today that threaten your ability to cope? Like Jesus, you will need to look beyond your current circumstances to the hope that is promised by God. Only with the help of the Holy Spirit can you do this. Spend time in the word filling your heart with the promises and hope of God so that you can look beyond your current situation.

All Power

*He canceled the record of the charges against us and
took it away by nailing it to the cross. In this way, he
disarmed the spiritual rulers and authorities. He shamed
them publicly by his victory over them on the cross.*

COLOSSIANS 2:13–15 NLT

Jesus had been beaten and He was weak; Simon carried His cross to
Calvary. "Along the way, they came across a man named Simon, who was
from Cyrene, and the soldiers forced him to carry Jesus' cross" (Matthew
27:32 NLT). Scriptures mercifully leave out the details of the horrible act
of crucifixion, even though we can read them in historical books and see
them in movies. On a hill outside the city Jesus was nailed to a cross, His
arms outstretched and His hands and feet pierced through with nails.
Although Jesus had been beaten beyond human weakness, His deity was
not lessened.

Two criminals were crucified with Him, one on His right side, one
on His left side. Symbolic of how the world will respond to Jesus, one
mocked Him, telling Jesus "If You are the Christ, save Yourself and us"
(Luke 23:39). The other criminal, aware of his own sin and repentant,
acknowledged the sinlessness of Jesus and submitted himself to Jesus
saying: "Jesus, remember me when you come into your Kingdom" (Luke
23:42 NLT). Jesus in His power and deity responded "Truly, I say to
you, today you will be with me in Paradise" (Luke 23:43 ESV). On the
cross, in His weakest human moment, Jesus, God with us, had the power
and chose to grant eternal life (John 5:21). He came to earth so that we
might live.

Jesus' time on earth was a statement of His deity, power and authority. When Pilate reminded Jesus of his power to make a judgment about crucifixion, Jesus reminded Pilate that his power was granted to him only from above (John 19:11). Speaking to the Pharisees earlier in His ministry, he let them know they had no power over Him. "Therefore My Father loves Me, because I lay down My life that I may take it again. No one takes it from Me, but I lay it down of Myself. I have power to lay it down, and I have power to take it again. This command I have received from My Father" (John 10:17–18). Even though He had all power, Jesus allowed and accepted every pain, every indignity and every blow to His body so we could be redeemed.

In His last display of pre-resurrection power, Jesus laid down His life, saying "It is finished!" And bowing His head, He gave up His spirit" (John 19:30). The Jewish leaders ignited His conviction, but no one took His life from Him; He voluntarily laid down His life for our redemption. The Good Shepherd laid down His life for His sheep. The work of redemption had been completed.

The power of nature was released at Jesus' death. Matthew 27:51–54 records that the veil of the temple was torn from top to bottom, rocks split, the earth quaked and graves were opened and saints were resurrected. One of the centurions responsible for guarding Jesus saw these signs and said "Truly this was the Son of God." Even His death was accompanied by belief and salvation. This is the power of our God and His gospel. Never dismiss the power that is inherent in sharing the gospel with others. Do your part in sharing and leave room for the Holy Spirit to work in the hearts of men.

All of the gifts we receive at salvation are made possible by one moment in time; the moment Jesus was crucified on our behalf. This was the moment that Satan thought he had defeated God and won the battle for His glory. This work was finished in the spiritual realm long before the founding of the earth because God ordained our redemption and He cannot lie. What looked like a horrible end to Jesus' ministry was just one more step in God's plan to redeem His people from their sin. Love did not die on the cross, it was magnified on the cross, and the time for Jesus to execute judgment came one step closer to Satan (John 5:26–-27).

* * *

Time in His Word:

Read John 5:22–-30; Colossians 2:11–15

Prayer:

Lord, Your word says the work of our redemption is finished. Yet, there are days when we keep trying to gain Your approval. We keep trying to finish a work that has already been done. Lord, quiet us. Help us to rest in Your promises and in Your eternal security. Jesus said "It is finished." Help us to rest in that and to call others to rest in this truth. Thank You Father that it is finished. In the name of Jesus Christ. Amen.

Meditations and Journaling:

This battle is over and done. Believe that God has rescued you from the kingdom of Satan. How do you honor that truth before others in your daily walk with God?

DAY 41

Meet Me in Galilee

I tell you the truth, you will weep and mourn
over what is going to happen to me, but
the world will rejoice. You will grieve, but your
grief will suddenly turn to wonderful joy.

JOHN 16:20 NLT

When I first started to watch Marvel Superhero movies, I did not understand that the movie was not over just because the credits rolled. When Jesus breathed His last breath and the centurions confirmed His death, for many the spectacle was over. The credits had rolled. "And all the crowds that had assembled for this spectacle, when they saw what had taken place, returned home beating their breasts. And all his acquaintances and the women who had followed him from Galilee stood at a distance watching these things" (Luke 23:48–49 ESV). Regardless of how it appeared to the rest of the world, for Jesus' followers, the movie was not over.

Death is final, or so it appears. Perhaps there would need to be a time of contemplation to understand what had just happened and what it meant for believers in Christ. Like John the Baptist, maybe His followers were left wondering if Jesus was the Messiah, or would another come. No doubt there would be grieving. For now, practical things needed to be taken care of; the bodies could not remain on the crosses through the Sabbath. Joseph of Arimathea came to take the body of Jesus for burial and Nicodemus came bearing spices to anoint the body. Jesus was prepared for burial and laid in a new tomb and a stone rolled over the tomb to cover the entrance. The women watched to see where they laid Him (Luke 23:50-55). Many were left wondering what phenomenon had rocked their world over the past three years. Was the truth that caused their hearts to burn within them just for a time? Was it over?

In all that had happened over the past two days, there was hardly time to consider and remember all that Jesus told His disciples at the Last Supper. Did they forget the one key statement He made to bolster their hope and allow them to walk away from Calvary knowing that His death was not final? Would they remember the one little nugget that would lessen their grief and shock over His death? Just before leaving the Upper Room headed to the garden of Gethsemane, Jesus said these words:" But after I have been raised from the dead, I will go ahead of you to Galilee and meet you there." (Matthew 26:32 NLT)

Did they forget? Have you forgotten the words that bring you hope?

* * *

Time in His Word:

Read Psalm 22

Prayer:

Our Father in heaven, hallowed be thy name. Thank You for Your Holy Spirit that brings all things to our remembrance when we need to hear from heaven. In our busyness and grief, help us not to turn a deaf ear to Your word and the hope that it brings. Let us hide Your word in our hearts so that You are always near and Your word lifts us. In the name of Jesus Christ. Amen.

Meditations and Journaling:

In the midst of life, do you often forget His words spoken to give you hope and help you remember that you are His beloved? How often do you sometimes find yourself in despair over circumstances because you choose not to go to the throne for rescue out of the dark places? What specific passage in the Bible lifts you up and restores your hope? Read that passage now and thank God for His care for you.

DAY 42

Risen Savior

*His name shall endure forever; His name shall
continue as long as the sun. And men shall be
blessed in Him; All nations shall call Him blessed.*

PSALMS 72:17

They did not leave for Galilee. Instead, they mourned and wept (Mark
16:10). They hid away in a room, afraid of the Jews (John 20:19). Mary
and others went to the tomb and encountered angels who proclaimed
the truth that Jesus is risen. Jesus appeared first to Mary Magdalene and
told her to go and tell the others and she did. Peter and John raced to the
tomb. "Then the disciple who had reached the tomb first also went in,
and he saw and believed—for until then they still hadn't understood the
Scriptures that said Jesus must rise from the dead. Then they went home"
(John 20:8–10 NLT). They still did not leave for Galilee. Was it all too
unreal, just too much?

Later that same evening Jesus appeared to the assembled disciples in
Jerusalem. Thomas was not with them. Jesus showed them His hands
and His side where He was pierced. When they told Thomas of Jesus'
appearance, Thomas doubted, saying he needed to see it for himself. Eight
days later in the same room, Jesus appeared again – for Thomas. Jesus
invited Thomas to touch him, to believe. "Then he said to Thomas, 'Put
your finger here, and look at my hands. Put your hand into the wound
in my side. Don't be faithless any longer. Believe!'" (John 20:27 NLT).
Thomas believed, proclaiming "My Lord and My God."

Later, Jesus reminded them of the words and prophecies He taught
them before the crucifixion. He reminded them that the prophecies He

spoke to them had to be fulfilled, that He had to be crucified and buried, but that He would rise from death. "Then he opened their minds to understand the Scriptures. And he said, "Yes, it was written long ago that the Messiah would suffer and die and rise from the dead on the third day. It was also written that this message would be proclaimed in the authority of his name to all the nations, beginning in Jerusalem: 'There is forgiveness of sins for all who repent.' You are witnesses of all these things" (Luke 24:45–48 NLT). Now, they understood. Now they could celebrate the risen Savior.

They didn't go to Galilee. Jesus came to them in Jerusalem. Thomas didn't believe when they told him of Jesus' appearance. Jesus came back for Thomas. They didn't understand all about the resurrection. Jesus opened their understanding and taught them. Jesus met them where they were – in Jerusalem, in their unbelief, in their misunderstanding. He will do the same for you. Wherever you are today, He will meet you and strengthen your unbelief and grow your faith. He will come to you if you ask.

We serve a risen Savior. We do not serve a fallible human who died and did not rise again. He has been given all power in heaven and on earth (Matthew 28:18). His resurrection is your divine guarantee that your salvation is secure. His resurrection is your guarantee that God has accepted Jesus' substitutionary death as atonement for our sins. His resurrection broke the power that sin holds over us. His resurrection broke the power of death for all believers, and is the guarantee of your resurrection. His resurrection put Satan on notice that his fate is secure and sealed. His resurrection is our reason for faith, the fulfillment of God's promises to each follower of Christ Jesus. The work of redemption is finished.

* * *

So Great A Love

Blessed be the God and Father of our Lord Jesus Christ! According to his great mercy, he has caused us to be born again to a living hope through the resurrection of Jesus Christ from the dead, to an inheritance that is imperishable, undefiled, and unfading, kept in heaven for you,

1 PETER 1:3–4 ESV

Jesus laid down His life for His friends. You are His friend if you know Him as Lord and Savior of your life, if you have chosen to follow Him. His death on the cross was an act of sacrificial, active, agape love. This was more than the love we have for our family, the love between a man and a woman, or the love between friends. Agape love seeks your highest good at all times. This is unconditional love. This is the love we all seek, but never know until we become friends with God. This is the love we search for and never find until we are reconciled to God through a relationship with Jesus Christ. This is the love we cannot share with others until we have experienced it with God ourselves.

From Genesis to Revelation in the Bible, God's sacrificial love is recorded. From the creation and covering of Adam and Eve to the resurrection, we see evidence of His love. Not for a moment of your life are you separated from His love. He knows the hairs on your head, and numbers the tears that you shed. Everything in your life is known to Him. He never stops seeking your highest good. The Psalmist says He is acquainted with all your ways (Psalm 139:3).

This is the love that restored Peter when he denied Jesus. This is the love that prayed for Peter before he even denied Jesus. This is the love that already knew that Peter would feed Jesus' sheep when he was restored. This is the love that watches over you and picks you up when you fail. This is the love that convicts, doesn't condemn, and walks you gently back onto the path of righteousness each day.

Because of God's love for you, Jesus was resurrected and ascended into heaven and sent His Holy Spirit to indwell each believer. In this active love, Jesus sits at the right hand of God and intercedes on behalf of each believer. "Therefore He is also able to save to the uttermost those who come to God through Him, since He always lives to make intercession for them" (Hebrews 7:25). Jesus died for you to be saved, He lives to work on your behalf!

It is this love for all mankind that urges each of us to tell others about Jesus. This sacrificial love promises each believer eternity with God in a new earth where there will be no more tears, no more sorrow, no more death. This active love promises us glorified bodies that will never wear out, replacing the ones that give us so much pain today.

God put Adam and Eve out of the garden of Eden and placed angels at its entrance to block the way to the tree of life so they would not eat of that tree and live forever in a state of sin. He sent Jesus to pay the price for our sin debt. For those who believe and accept the offer of life through Jesus, the tree of life is still available, offering the promise of eternity with God. The Apostle John recorded a vision of the trees of life in God's future paradise: "Then the angel showed me the river of the water of life, bright as crystal, flowing from the throne of God and of the Lamb through the middle of the street of the city; also, on either side of the river, the tree of life with its twelve kinds of fruit, yielding its fruit each month. The leaves of the tree were for the healing of the nations" (Revelation 22:1–2 ESV). Abundant life for each of us.

God desires to heal you completely with His love. Will you accept that invitation?

HOW WILL YOU RESPOND?

For God so loved the world that He gave His only begotten Son, that
whoever believes in Him should not perish but have everlasting life.
John 3:16

What will you do in the face of a love this great, a love for you, poured out at Calvary? Such an act of love calls for a response. His love always carries an invitation to enter in. Enter into His family, enter into hope, enter into the promise of eternity with Him.

How will you respond? His love toward you is undying, unrelenting, unchanging, unconditional, and unremitting. His love is for whoever chooses to come to Him and lay down the burdens of this life and enter into His rest. What will you do? Today is the day of your choice. Will you say "Yes, Lord," or will you respond with a shrug of your shoulders and walk away? Will you put off deciding until another day?

God does not need your riches, your promises, or your earthly goods. Everything is His. He desires your heart, your life, your obedience. In fact, we have nothing but ourselves to give. As long as you are alive and breathing, you can respond to His offer of love. The offer of eternity expires when you close your eyes in death. Tomorrow is not promised to any of us. Today is the day of decision.

Remember Hannah, the wife of Elkanah, who prayed for a child? When Hannah petitioned the Lord to end her season of barrenness, she promised that child to the Lord before she even became pregnant. "And she vowed a vow and said, "O Lord of hosts, if you will indeed look on the affliction of your servant and remember me and not forget your servant, but will give to your servant a son, then I will give him to the Lord all the days of his life, and no razor shall touch his head" (1 Samuel 1:11 ESV). Faithful to her promise, she brought Samuel to the temple to serve the Lord as soon as she weaned him. Her gratefulness to the Lord knew no bounds and she offered to God what she valued most. Despite Hannah's heart of gratitude, it later had to be Samuel's decision to faithfully follow the Lord all the days of his life. Falling in love with Jesus is an individual decision.

Sometimes what we value most are the things of this world and He has no desire for those things. What He desires is your heart, sold out to Him in love and obedience. Give Him your life today and watch His love spill out toward you in abundance as you grow in relationship with Him. Draw near and feel the warmth of His love in your life as He guides you and leads you. Today is your day.

How will you respond?

FINAL THOUGHTS

Thank you for spending these days with my words searching out God's love for you. My prayer and my hope are that you have been restored and confirmed in your faith in God as you read these pages. I pray that you will choose to know Him deeply and more intimately than ever before. I pray that you will allow Him to impact your heart and change your life for His glory. I have been privileged to write these words and to pray for you.

There comes a day of reckoning for each of us, a day when we either hit rock bottom, or just become tired of despair dogging our lives. I spent many years in depression and despair, searching and trying different outlets looking for happiness. When I was forty, I was facing major surgery and I was scared. One thought kept running through my mind: I need to get right with God. I honestly can tell you that thought was not something anyone told me; I believe it was God wooing me. I absolutely knew that I would not go into surgery without taking care of that issue, even though I did not know exactly what that meant.

One Sunday I got up, put on a yellow dress and went to church alone. I'm not sure what I expected, but I had passed this particular church for years and I felt that was where I needed to go, so I did. I was late because I didn't know what time services started. I slipped into a seat in the last pew and listened with amazement as the minister described my life: the searching, the despair, the need. When he finished his sermon, he asked everyone to bow their heads and close their eyes. He then asked if there was anyone there who did not know they would go to heaven if they died that night. I raised my hand, opened my eyes and peeked and was amazed no other hands were raised. But I did not put my hand down. I didn't know what I needed, but this felt right. Two ladies came and invited me to a room where they shared the story of Jesus birth, death, burial and resurrection – for me, for my sins. They offered me the opportunity to pray and accept that free gift offered by Jesus to pay my sin debt. I prayed for forgiveness and I have never looked back. It was the most significant moment in my life. I was right with God.

I could not have known on that day that it would go beyond knowing I would go to heaven when I died. One of the saddest things for me is when I encounter a Christian who only wants eternity with God. That is sad because I have learned over these past years how much He wants to love you and walk with you in this life, not just the next life. I would run out of words trying to tell you the adventure that is walking with Christ each day. My life changed; my outlook changed. There are still days when I am depressed, but I know without a doubt that He is with me each day and I only have to put me and my situations into His hand to find release. He will not force anything; He desires your willing submission to Him. I have what I can only describe as wholeness; I am complete. I am no longer searching. I have the joy of knowing hope in any situation. I pray the same (and more) for you. I pray for you to know joy.

If you would like to share any thoughts with me about this book or your journey toward Jesus, feel free to contact me via email at epicjourney_olivia@att.net; or you can contact me on Facebook (Olivia Davenport, author). I look forward to hearing how God is stirring your soul with His love.

Be blessed.
Live in His presence.
Know that He loves you.

MY SONG OF PRAISE*

LORD, I was lost, wandering and wondering
You reached out, took my hand
And here we are, these many days later
You lead, I follow; sometimes I complain
We go places, always together
Sometimes I wander off
You wait for me, but You are with me.
You are there when I return;
You didn't leave me
You chastise me in love
You walk with me when I am in danger
You carry me when I can't go any farther
You heal my Spirit
You heal my body
You alone are worthy!
You alone are the One I run to
It is You that my soul misses when I am absent
Abba, my Father, I love You.
I thank You above all
I praise You
I honor You
I love You
I glorify You
In the name of my Savior Jesus, Your Mediator
Amen

---

* See Meditations, page 15

And this is His commandment: that we should believe on the name of His Son Jesus Christ and love one another, as He gave us commandment.

1 JOHN 3:23

ENDNOTES

1   See Genesis 17:8; Exodus 6:7; Jeremiah 32:38; Ezekiel 14;11; Zechariah 8:8; 2 Corinthians 6:16; Hebrews 8:10; Revelation 21:3,7.